Greg,

Don't drink too much of this stuff but when you do... consider yourself educated on it !!! Happy 21<u>st</u> !

Love Always,
Sommer

GILBERT DELOS

VODKAS
of the
WORLD

Photographs by Matthieu Prier

© Copyright Paris 1998
This edition published in North America by
WELLFLEET PRESS
a division of Book Sales Inc.
114 Northfield Avenue
Edison, New Jersey 08837
ISBN: 0-7858-1018-8

Editorial coordinator: Nicolas Jeanneau
Cover photo: Matthieu Prier
Lay-out : Nicole Leymarie
Cover design: Copyright Studio (Hervé Tardy and Ute-Charlotte Hettler)
Translation: Heidi Ellison

GILBERT DELOS

VODKAS
of the
WORLD

Photographs by Matthieu Prier

THE WELLFLEET PRESS

CONTENTS

6
THE HISTORY OF VODKA
The spirit that came in from the cold

14
THE MAKING OF VODKA
Purity vs. flavor

22
LES VODKAS RUSSES
Russia: a national symbol, 23
Styles and brands, 34
Smirnoff: up and down in history, 52

60
POLISH VODKAS
Poland: authenticity and diversity, 60
Styles and brands, 72

88

SCANDINAVIAN VODKAS
Scandinavia: purity meets Puritanism, 89
Swedish vodkas, 90
Absolut, 100
Finnish vodkas, 108
Danish vodkas, 118
Norwegian vodkas, 120
Baltic vodkas, 122

124

AQUAVIT

134

THE REST OF THE WORLD

144

ENJOYING VODKA
Traditional uses, 146
Vodka cocktails, 152

158

INDEX

THE SPIRIT THAT CAME IN FROM THE COLD

Vodka originated in Northern Europe and comes in a variety of forms that vary greatly according to their provenance, raw materials, and production methods, and the traditions of different countries.

"Vodka" is, in fact, a generic term. In both the Russian and Polish languages (the latter also uses *woda*), it is a diminutive of the world *voda*, which means "water"; thus "vodka" means simply "little water." It is, in a way, water that has been reduced by distillation, or perhaps by freezing, during the first phase of its production.

The term itself was not immediately used when the drink made its first appearance in Northern Europe at the beginning of the sixteenth century; it came into common use only a century or two later. It probably spread in Russia, where it designated a spirit that was distilled at least twice (but often more), based primarily on grains, but also on other raw materials like potatoes or molasses. Flavor could be added in a variety of ways.

Stolichnaya and Moskovskaya are the most representative Moscow vodkas. The drink helps warm frosty nights in northern climes like that shown above.

Unlike other spirits, including whiskey, cognac, and gin, this vague definition was never really codified, either in terms of production method or provenance. Since the fall of communism, Russia has been trying to take back control of the word "vodka," but it has taken on its own meanings all around the world. The white alcohols known as "vodka" that are made industrially just about everywhere and sport vaguely Russianized labels have hardly any resemblance to the original product.

Vodka has become a fashionable drink popular for its ability to be mixed with other ingredients. As shown by its bottles, packaging, and advertising, it has become an unequaled springboard for creative imaginations.

MEDICINAL PROPERTIES

As is true of most spirits, the exact origin of vodka is unknown. Writings and historical proofs are lacking, and its beginnings were marked by only the occasional successful experimentation.

The technique of distillation was used for many centuries before it was really perfected; certainly humans have been familiar with fermented drinks for thousands of years. The most ancient traces found to date attest to the manufacture of beer in Jericho as far back as 6000 B.C. Since then, we have evidence of vineyards and the production of other fermented beverages such as cider, palm wine, and sake.

However, these beverages involved only natural fermentation; the sugars contained in the fruits and grains were transformed into alcohol once a certain temperature was reached.

The principle of distillation was not discovered and the first primitive stills were not built until much later. This was mostly the work of Arab doctors–before the year 1000–who were looking for ways of preserving the beneficial properties of plants and other ingredients used as medicines at the time. By marinating their medicines in fermented liquids, usually wine, then heating them in closed vessels, they eventually obtained liqueurs and potions with great longevity. This was simple distillation, which resulted in an alcohol content of only twenty to thirty percent by volume.

The research continued during the Middle Ages, and was conducted by alchemists such as Raymond Lulle and Paracelsus and scholars in the Italian city of Salerno, a meeting place for doctors from the Arab and Christian worlds. In Montpellier in the thirteenth century, the Catalan Arnaud de Villeneuve was

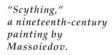

"Scything,"
a nineteenth-century
painting by
Massoiedov.

one of the first to use the term *eau-de-vie*, which he intended for external use. And, in the abbeys that were spreading across Europe, the monks were also experimenting with recipes for elixirs and liqueurs of all kinds. While these concoctions were sometimes used for their own consumption, the monks were actually searching for new medicines.

It was only in the Netherlands at the beginning of the sixteenth century that distillation was used exclusively for purposes of consumption. This is not at all surprising since the Dutch were the best sailors of the period and had discovered that with distilled, or "burnt," wine (*bramwinj* in Flemish, the origin of the word "brandy"), they had a drink that traveled well and provided a solution to the problem of the conservation of water.

The first distilleries of the modern era were set up in Schiedam, in the suburbs of Rotterdam. They used mostly wine, especially from Charente in France, which led to the creation of cognac. There are some earlier writings that mention the existence of distilleries in other countries, notably in Armagnac, but these were isolated cases that did not necessarily have much promise of a future.

Northern Europeans knew about distillation techniques for the making of medicine at a fairly early date. In the fifteenth century, for example, there is evidence of a visit by members by the Russian church to Italy, where they learned the basics of distillation at a monastery.

Later, around 1534, in Poland, Stefan Falimirz published a treatise entitled "On Herbs and Their Properties." In it, he explained that "vodkas can be burned or distilled, with the addition of herbs, spices, and mixtures of herbs and flowers. . . . They can also be extracted from fruits, berries, juniper, and laurel." But it is probable that these preparations contained little alcohol. They were used as external unguents to soothe pain, as potions, or even as aftershaves– the treatise speaks of using "vodka to wash the chin after shaving it."

In addition to these documented facts, there are many legends concerning the origins of vodka. One of them claims that it originated during the great freezes that occurred in Russia. Water freezes before alcohol, allowing the further concentration of the initial alcoholic

"Saint Petersburg Seen from Vassiliev Island," an eighteenth-century engraving. In the foreground, workers are drinking vodka.

drink and creating a stronger preparation if the excess ice is removed before the alcohol freezes. This is a chancy operation, however, and the results would be of uncertain quality; nor has any document attested to such a practice, at least on a scale large enough to justify its claim to be the original vodka.

THE BEGINNING OF INDUSTRIALIZATION

The first Dutch *eaux-de-vie* were distilled primarily from wine (Dutch traders knew

Above: "Parisian Peace," an engraving by Graviliatchenko. Russian Cossacks are celebrating the victory over Napoléon.

where to procure sufficient quantities of it, notably in France). Wine also produced a better quality of alcohol than grains, which were reserved for human and animal consumption or for the making of beer. When there were shortages of grains, the brewers were deprived of their supplies.

The opposite was true in other Northern European countries, where the climate was hardly suitable for growing vines, aside from southern Poland, where there were some attempts at distillation, and in Georgia. Importing sufficient quantities of wine was much too expensive.

Grains, however, were abundant, especially rye, which was already being used to make a light beer called *kvas*, and provided an interesting raw material that could be distilled several times. There were also plenty of forests to supply all the wood needed to heat the stills. But distilling methods were still primitive, and the resulting alcohol was not always of high quality. The spirits obtained were often full of noxious elements, not only in terms of taste but also for health, such as methanol.

The first distillers did not rely exclusively on grains to fill their stills; they used almost anything that nature had to offer as long as it contained sugars that could be fermented, including all types of fruits, or starches that could be transformed into sugar, like potatoes.

To add flavor to these sometimes tasteless raw materials, it became a common practice,

Right: The Lancut Museum in Poland houses a few marvels, including this superb, perfectly preserved still dating to the first half of the nineteenth century.

especially in Poland, to macerate herbs, plants, roots, orange peel, pits, berries, and other ingredients in the vodka after distillation.

These vodkas had different flavors and degrees of alcohol (some were distilled five times or even more). They were all enormously popular, to the point of becoming part of the national culture, especially in Russia. In the cold northern climes, vodka's ability to warm people faster than other alcoholic beverages made it very welcome, all the more so because it was relatively inexpensive. It is not surprising then that many states quickly found it in their best interest to encourage the development of vodka. And, because consumption was so widespread, it became an obvious source of revenue. Manufacturing monopolies soon appeared, many of them belonging to the ruling classes, aristocrats, and upper middle classes, who were being rewarded for their loyalty to·the monarch. Later, state monopolies took control of the manufacture and distribution of alcohol, even in the non-communist states of Scandinavia.

FURTHER REFINEMENTS

The consumption of vodka continued to increase, and in the nineteenth century two

important innovations were introduced: charcoal filtering and the continuous still.

Charcoal filtering, after many experiments, proved to be the best way of filtering vodka to remove many of its impurities and bad tastes. The procedure, invented in Russia and developed primarily by Piotr Smirnov (founder of the company later known in the West as Smirnoff), allowed the making of a more refined beverage with a purer flavor and fewer harmful ingredients.

In addition, after a series of improvements to the still–many of them based on the work of the Frenchman Chaptal–, a new technique revolutionized the world of spirits. The continuous still, based on the research of the Frenchman Cellier-Blumenthal and the Scot Coffey, was invented in the first half of the nineteenth century.

In the earlier system, which is still used to make cognac in Charente and malt whiskey in Scotland, the still was a heated tank that had to be refilled once the raw material (wine or mash) was treated. This requires great care and nearly constant attention. The first and last parts–the head and tail– of the distilled liquid must be eliminated each time because they contain too many noxious elements. Only the middle part, called the "heart," is kept.

The continuous still eliminates all these steps as it functions nonstop once it is filled with the raw materials. Productivity is thus much higher since high degrees of alcohol can be achieved faster.

The resulting vodka is rather different because many desirable flavors are lost in the process; the alcohol is more neutral in taste but is purer. Since it cost less to make and sell, however, it was an attractive option, and the continuous still quickly spread all over Northern Europe, replacing the type used in

Charente, with the exception of a few artisans who continued to use the traditional methods.

REVOLUTIONARY CHANGES

The Russian Revolution in 1917 and the Soviet domination of Poland and the Baltic countries, beginning in 1945, completely changed the way vodka was produced, sold, and consumed.

In the early days, the Russian revolutionaries took an ideological stance; they declared alcohol a pernicious influence and tried to halt its production. The major producers were quickly nationalized and their assets seized. The Smirnov distillery, the largest in Moscow, was turned into a state garage.

But production resumed fairly soon in response to strong demand. Clandestine distilleries began to make vodkas of dubious quality, some of them dangerous to the drinker's health. Vodka was still an important part of the national culture, however, and ten years after the Revolution, the communists took over its production.

But the Soviet bureaucracy was not capable of creating the type of brand image that was developing in the capitalist world in the twentieth century. The Russian consumer had a choice between different styles of vodka, but

ABSOLUT ATTRACTION.

Soviet world. The Americans, followed by the rest of the Western world, began to take an interest in vodka. This was led by Smirnoff, which had been renamed to stress its Russian origins, since, during the height of the Cold War, czarist Russia had become popular.

At a time when the Soviets seemed incapable of protecting their national heritage, the major alcohol producers of the United States and Britain began to make vodka, or at least industrially produced grain alcohol.

Transparent and nearly tasteless, these beverages became increasingly popular in the marketplace, thanks primarily to their ability to be mixed with almost any other ingredient. The vodkas that were used here did not have much in common with the original product, but a vaguely Russian name and label were enough to attract the masses, who cared little about where or how such products were made, especially since there were few consumers who knew anything about the real thing. Poland, which had continued more or less without interruption to make its flavored vodkas in the traditional way, was the only exception. It exported its vodka, and Zubrowka, perfumed with buffalo grass, became well known. But enlarging the market for perfumed vodkas was difficult since they were nothing like the popular version. They were drunk straight and well-chilled, preferably with a meal, and were not meant to be mixed with orange or tomato juice.

nothing made one stand out from the others. The great brands that had begun to make the reputation of Russian vodka in the time of the czars, including Smirnov, were abandoned without a thought.

After World War II, a new phenomenon occurred that, oddly enough, did not affect the

Below: Bottling at the Cristall distillery in Moscow.

A FASHION PHENOMENON

Unlike the makers of other spirits such as whiskey and rum, which flaunted their roots and their specific flavors, the international vodka brands could hardly make such claims. They found another way to advertise their product: for its purity and originality.

The Swedish brand Absolut provides the best example. Thanks to its highly creative advertising campaigns, this vodka that claimed to be the purest of all saw astonishing growth and became a fashion phenomenon. By associating with the most innovative artists, the most inventive designers and the best-known photographers, it became the "must" drink at fashion shows, trendy nightclubs and upscale art gallery openings. The Swedish origins of the vodka have been conveniently forgotten, except when used to prove that it was above all not a Soviet product.

Other Scandinavian vodkas, like Finlandia, followed the same path and have been joined more recently by other neutral-tasting vodkas from North America and Western Europe (the Netherlands, Germany, and Italy). Detached from their heritage, they are conceived as entirely separate creations, and the word "vodka" has become just another term that provides access to the lucrative shelves of major stores. The winner is the brand that comes in the most original bottle in terms of its shape or label design, and has the most startling advertising campaign and the most striking argument to publicize its name. Only the container matters; the contents are an afterthought, as long as they are sufficiently flavorless.

Since the fall of communism at the end of the 1980s, the original producers, primarily the Russians, have been trying to regain control of a phenomenon that slipped out of their hands more than a half-century ago. From the sidelines, they had watched the popularization and globalization of a product that is one of the foundations of their culture. Today they are reclaiming their ownership rights to the word "vodka." They would have us believe that the only good vodka is a Russian vodka; all others are imitations that don't measure up to the original. The descendants of Piotr

Smirnov who still live in Russia have even gone to court to try to regain ownership rights to the Smirnoff brands.

But it is now too late for the original vodkas. Today, there are even Internet sites devoted to all types of vodka. Champagne, cognac, bourbon, and Scotch whiskey were able to preserve their reputations by preventing imitations that tried to take advantage of the fame of the original product, but those battles have been going on for decades, and some for a century.

Vodka has spread so thoroughly throughout the world that it is difficult to see how protective international legislation could possibly reserve the use of the name to Northern European producers.

Left and facing page, top: The striking and unusual Absolut advertising campaign uses only the image of the bottle and a one- or two-word slogan.

PURITY VS. FLAVOR

The art of making spirits always involves a compromise between optimal purity and the maintenance or enhancement of specific flavors provided by the raw materials. Not only does vodka not escape this problem, but it is also the alcohol that best illustrates it, since the term "vodka" covers a variety of different products, ranging from pure and practically tasteless alcohols to others with strong flavors. There are also vodkas that have multiple flavors.

For the historical reasons explained in the preceding chapter, vodka was never the subject of precise classification, unlike most other spirits, whether in terms of raw materials, distillation techniques, or types of added flavors. With vodka, anything is possible.

Lancut, one of the oldest distilleries in Poland, was set up on the vast lands of the Lubomirski family. Today, the most up-to-date techniques are used to rectify and bottle the vodka.

Above and facing page: Harvesting in southern Sweden and near Moscow. Almost any grain can be used in the production of vodka.

THE CHOICE OF RAW MATERIALS

Grains, especially rye, are the most common raw material for traditional vodka. These grasses are highly resistant to cold and can grow in poor soil, and are thus especially well-adapted to the rough weather conditions of Northern European countries. Used for the making of bread, grains also supply the base for *kvas,* the light beer whose mash is used to make the highest quality Russian vodkas.

But almost any other grain can also be used in the manufacture of vodka, including wheat,

barley, millet, and corn. Other plants containing the required amounts of sugar (or fermentable starches) that are transformable into alcohol–such as potatoes, beets, apples, onions, carrots, and pumpkins–can also provide a base for vodka, as can molasses, a by-product of the crystallization of refined sugar. Most of these ingredients, however, are rarely used; today, most vodka is made of grains, potatoes, or molasses.

The potato is often looked down upon, a vestige of the days when it was cheap and often used to make clandestine vodka. This is no longer true, even though the yields from

Vodka is rarely made from just one ingredient, and if it is, it is usually rye, or at least exclusively grains.

The other essential ingredient is water. It is not surprising that vodkas from the Moscow region have long had a reputation for quality, since its water is especially soft, with little sediment and few mineral salts. It gives the vodkas made there greater finesse. Today, we know how to soften water, but, depending on the location, the procedure is more or less costly, and many producers do not take the trouble to make sure the water they use is of high enough quality.

Water is used in two main stages of vodka making. It is first mixed with raw materials in the form of flour or pulp to create the mash, the holy mixture that will then follow the path of distillation. It is also used in large quantities in the final stage to lower the degree of alcohol in the spirits coming out of the still.

The role played by water in the final characteristics of the vodka is illustrated by the production of the Polmos group, the largest manufacturer in Poland. While the same recipe is used to make the group's leading vodkas, specialists can detect differences depending on which of the company's twenty-five distilleries they were made in.

THE IMPORTANCE OF DISTILLATION

The mash obtained from different raw materials (grains or other plants) must first

grains are two or three times higher than from potatoes: one hundred kilograms of potatoes makes slightly less than ten liters of alcohol, while the same weight in grains makes up to thirty liters. The potato is nonetheless an excellent base for vodka. In Poland, regular selection has led to the cultivation of special varieties of potatoes that make vodkas with fine aromas. Their starch content, which is transformed into sugar by fermentation, is up to twice that of varieties used for human or animal consumption.

These raw materials are often combined, depending mostly on price fluctuations.

In addition, some cereal varieties, such as hard wheat, contain too much gluten and not enough starch. If they are used in the making of the mash, the unusable gluten must be removed during distillation.

The search for maximum purity, which avoids all noxious effects, led distillers to make vodkas that were increasingly neutral, especially after the development of the continuous still in the second half of the nineteenth century. It sometimes happens today that vodkas are made containing less than thirty milligrams of aromatic materials per liter, compared with more than two thousand milligrams per liter in other spirits like cognac. The Swedish vodka Absolut, which boasts that it is the purest possible, nevertheless contains a small amount of less-distilled alcohol that gives it a hint of flavor.

Such vodkas are distilled several times–two or three times for most, but some distillers go even further. One American vodka supposedly undergoes six successive distillations.

On the other side of the fence are the smaller distillers who continue to use pot stills (the type used in Charente) to obtain more flavorful vodkas that carry an aromatic reminder of their raw materials.

While the term vodka encompasses spirits that vary greatly, they do have one point in common that has nothing to do with flavor and which distinguishes them from other spirits made from grains or tubers. British gin, German schnapps, and Scandinavian aquavit are made from neutral alcohol, which is then flavored with spices or plants and distilled once more.

This is never done with vodka. When there is flavoring, it is always added after the final distillation and concerns only a simple maceration of the aromatic substances in the spirits. The difference may seem small, but it does play a role in better preserving the taste of the raw materials used.

Water, the essential ingredient in the making of vodka, is used at two stages: it is mixed with the basic raw materials and is used to lower the degree of the alcohol when it comes out of the still.

FILTRATION AND AGING

To eliminate unpleasant tastes, vodka distillers can use filtration techniques. In the past, they used such materials as vegetable fibers, sand, or felt, but better results were obtained when the Russians had the idea of using charcoal, which is much more absorbent than most other materials. Smirnov vodka built its reputation on the success of its charcoal filtering in the nineteenth century.

The oldest method used to eliminate

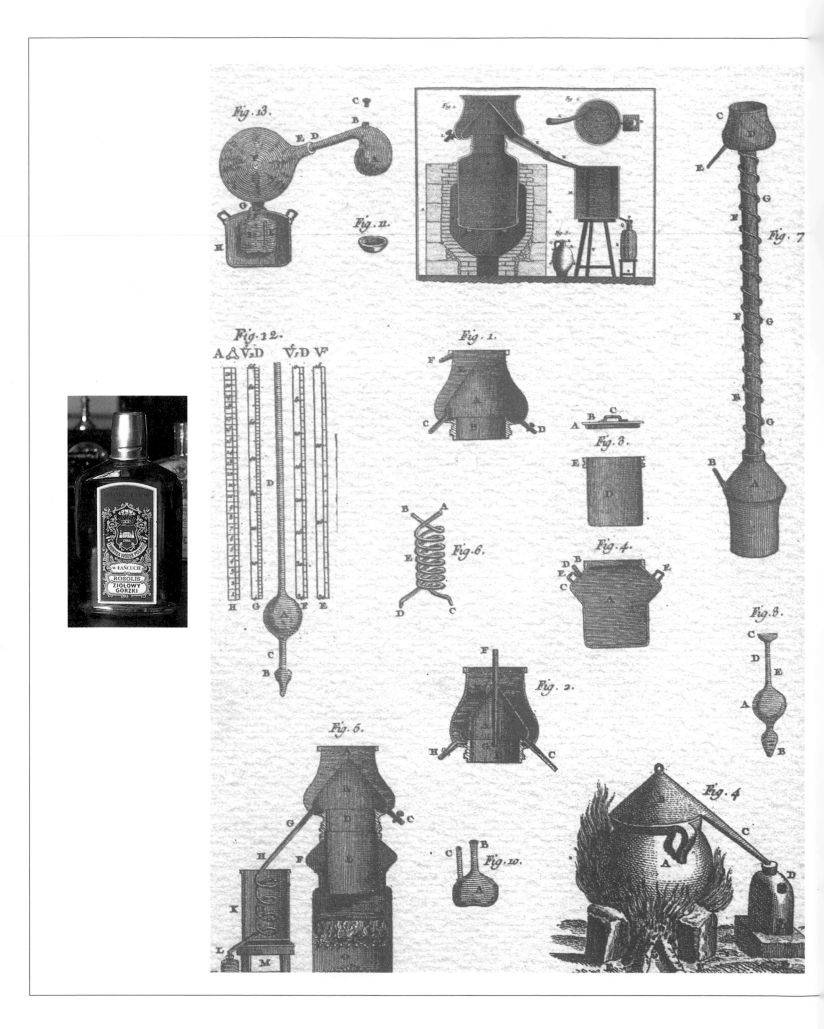

unpleasant flavors from vodka was to mask them by adding all sorts of aromatic substances: fruits, plants, spices, and so on. This led to the invention of a particular style of vodka that is most highly developed in Poland and Russia.

Two methods are used for flavoring vodka:

- The maceration of aromatic ingredients in vodkas of varying strengths for several weeks. Various methods, often kept secret, are used to achieve the maximum concentration of flavors in order to adjust the final degree of alcohol.

- A more recent technique consists of passing the alcohol several times through a filter containing aromatic substances. This method is faster and more economical and produces similar results.

Aromatic oils, which might be synthetic, can also be used to quickly add a particular flavor to a mostly neutral vodka. This industrial technique produces flavored vodkas of lower quality than those made with more traditional procedures.

Unlike many other spirits, such as whiskey, rum, or cognac, vodka is rarely aged for long periods. We have no historical explanation for this. There was always plenty of wood in Northern Europe for the making of barrels, and the technique had been used for a long time in many countries.

We can only assume that, since vodka was made to be drunk right away, no one ever took the time to see what would happen if it were aged for several years. In addition, this was a costly operation, and most producers did not have the financial means to wait ten or twenty years for the alcohol to age.

It must be noted, however, that a few producers, especially in Poland, leave their vodka in barrels for a time to develop certain added flavors, taking care not to use new barrels as it would add the flavor of new wood to the alcohol.

The Russian and Polish Starkas (which means "old") are known for their sweet, fruity flavor, the result of the addition of liqueur wines like malaga, and they are also flavored with various plants. They are barrel-aged for up to ten years, not to take on the flavor of the wood, but to better concentrate the aromas of the added ingredients. This would lead us to conclude that aging is simply not part of the culture of vodka, unlike that of cognac or whiskey.

RUSSIA:
A NATIONAL SYMBOL

For nearly five centuries, vodka has been an important part of the Russian national identity, a more representative symbol than balalaikas, dachas, and zakuski. Although there is no irrefutable proof that vodka was first made in Russia, it is certain that it was quickly adopted there and continues to be the most popular alcoholic beverage.

This symbol of national pride also has a more sinister flip side. Alcoholism and its ravages have caused much damage to the people under all the different regimes. Now that the country is beginning to develop a market economy, the Russians want to take back control of this beverage that has become known around the world. The Russians claim that the only good vodka is a Russian vodka, the others being at best only pale copies of the real thing and at worst just plain bad. This late wake-up call, which does not take into account the realities of the end of the twentieth century, demonstrates Russia's strong attachment to its national drink. The widespread conviction that vodka is a Russian drink is confirmed by the choice of Russian-sounding names by most foreign vodka producers when they have created a new brand.

Above and left: The Smirnov factory in Moscow.

Embroidered depiction of a feast during Ivan the Terrible's reign.

In 988, Vladimir I, known as the "Ardent Sun," converted to the Orthodox religion because, according to legend, Islam did not tolerate the consumption of alcohol. In founding the grand duchy of Kiev several years earlier, this prince had established the base of what would later become Russia and, at the same time, supplied the first symbol of the attachment of the region's people to alcoholic beverages, even though only beer, wine, and mead were known at the time.

The distillation of spirits was introduced several centuries later, probably by traders from the Baltic or by monks who had been initiated into the art, valued for its medical properties.

It is possible that the Russians had begun to master this technique with the exploitation of their forests' resin. To obtain the pitch, they heated logs of pine and other resinous woods in covered pits, a sort of primitive distillation process that released alcoholic vapors. They later transferred this method to fermented beverages like beer, especially *kvas,* made with rye.

«Vodka» was not the first name given to spirits in Russia: those made from beer or mead were called *perevera,* and those made from wine were known as *korchna.*

While there are some indications that Russian spirits were being exported to Scandinavia as early as the beginning of the sixteenth century, the first historical proofs of the existence of vodka date to the reign of Ivan the Terrible, prince of Russia, who was crowned czar in 1547. The founder of the Russian Empire quickly understood the possible financial interest of vodka; at the very beginning of his reign, he set up a monopoly for the distillation of the beverage, following the policy of his grandfather Ivan III, who had already developed a protectionist policy for the fledgling country. Ivan the Terrible opened the first cabarets in Moscow, called kabaki, where vodka from his distilleries was served.

This policy of monopolistic control over vodka remained a constant in the history of Russia, although the czars sometimes agreed to share with powerful lords or rich merchants to ensure their loyalty. The revenues provided by vodka quickly became very important as consumption grew at impressive rates, at times representing up to two-fifths of the state's revenues.

But there was another side to this monopolistic policy. It also led to bootlegging, a scourge that was never put to end. Those who could not or would not buy the state vodka quickly learned to distill it themselves, using all sorts of raw materials. The resulting spirits were often of mediocre quality and sometimes unhealthy, as they frequently contained methanol.

In addition, revolts often started in taverns, particularly in the seventeenth century, in protest against both the heavy taxes on the consumption of vodka, which led to the accumulation of unpayable debts, and against the taverns' poor-quality vodkas, made from potatoes or beets.

TO EACH HIS OWN VODKA

Russia always had different types of vodkas

for different social classes. The most refined (and the most expensive) were made from rye, sometimes with the addition of a small amount of other grains, such as barley or oats. At first, these cereals were used because they were recovered from the residue of flour mills, but later they were used because of the specific aromatic qualities they gave the vodka.

These high-quality vodkas were mostly consumed by aristocrats and rich merchants. During the eighteenth century, a time when the Russian elite was fascinated by Western Europe, and especially by France, the choice of vodka provided the country with a way of affirming its national and cultural identity.

Peter the Great, who unified the empire between the seventeenth and eighteenth centuries, was responsible for the widespread Westernization of his country. Nevertheless, during his frequent trips to Amster-

Above: "The Great Theater of Saint Petersburg," a nineteenth-century engraving by B. Paterson. Below: "The Writer Count Alexis Tolstoy Pays a Visit to the Painter," by Kontchalovsky (1941).

ing the number of distillations, which were performed slowly in small stages. They also sought improved filtration methods, such as the use of charcoal, which necessitated the lowering of the alcohol content by the addition of water, since charcoal could not purify an overly strong spirit.

Another solution was to coagulate the impurities with the help of fresh black bread, egg whites (a technique that is still used in the making of fine wines, especially in Bordeaux), whole eggs, ashes, or potash.

All of these improvements resulted in increasingly pure, transparent vodkas that represented the top of the range beginning in the second half of the nineteenth century. The increasing use of the continuous still at this time only accentuated the trend.

The chemist Dmitry Mendeleyev, known primarily for his periodic table of the elements, also took an interest in vodka. The subject of his doctoral thesis was the mixing of alcohol and water. After months of research on the ideal proportions, his formula included a total of thirty different elements. In his eyes, the perfect mix was achieved with 45.88 percent pure alcohol and 54.12 percent water! In practice, the percentage of alcohol in weight is around forty percent for both vodka and other spirits. This should not be confused with the volume measurement, which gives a slightly different proportion since alcohol is lighter than water.

The less-privileged social classes were content with much rougher vodkas made from potatoes or beets. Rapidly distilled and poorly purified, they were sold in bulk, the unit of measure being a bucket with a capacity of 12.3 liters. Refinement and purity did not come into play here. The important thing was that the vodka provided the necessary warmth and comfort to people suffering from the rigors of the climate and the penuries of their existence.

REVOLUTIONARY TORMENT

The takeover by the Bolsheviks in 1917 not only overthrew the czarist regime and its social organization, but also changed the history of vodka. The revolutionaries considered that vodka had a stupefying effect on the masses, and they quickly did all they could to

Above: A poster designed by Alexis Rutschkowski for Boyard vodka. Below: Nikita Khrushchev and Fidel Castro drink to friendship, an example of vodka helping to oil the wheels of diplomacy.

dam, London, and Germany, he always took his own vodka with him. When his supplies ran out, he plunged into misery because he had to drink cognac or other local spirits. He had a strong preference for vodka that had been distilled three times, then flavored with essence of anise. During his reign, he even became involved in distilling himself and perfected a type of still.

The Russian elite's taste for highly refined vodka led distillers to make continual improvements in order to eliminate unpleasant or undesirable flavors, either masking them with flavorings extracted from local plants and spices–and later imported ones–or by increas-

eradicate it (inasmuch as alcoholism threatened their own troops–during the siege of the Winter Palace in Saint Petersburg, many of the Bolshevik soldiers were too drunk to participate in the final charge, and a single Finnish regiment had to fight off the looters trying to make off with the contents of the czar's cellars.

Beginning in 1918, distilleries were confiscated and even dismantled, including that of the Smirnov family. Located in the heart of Moscow, it was transformed into a state garage. Until the middle of the 1930s, it was forbidden to produce beverages, whether beer or vodka, that contained more than twenty percent alcohol.

This revolutionary purity did not last, and ancestral habits quickly got the upper hand, all the more so since Stalin's reign of terror

was more acceptable to a people drowning in vodka. It was even reintroduced into soldiers' rations during World War II, a privilege that was not taken away until the war was over.

Like their predecessors, the czars, the communists found that vodka offered great financial advantages, even though they kept the price of ordinary vodka relatively low. It was sold in a large bottle with no cork, just a metal cap that was thrown away as soon as the bottle was opened (an open bottle was habitually drunk within a few hours).

Alcoholism was the hidden face of communism, and it took on immense proportions, although it was never officially recognized. The problem became patent in the final years of the Soviet regime: Leonid Brezhnev was often drunk, and Kon-

This old muzhik seems indifferent to the repressive measures taken by the Bolshevik regime.

Times have changed, and vodka has now become a promotional tool in Russia. Here, the recent launch of Jirinovski vodka is being celebrated.

stantin Chernenko, one of his successors in the post of secretary-general of the Communist Party, died of cirrhosis of the liver. Every sector of society was affected by the abuse of vodka, including the army. The Mig 25, the pride of the Soviet air force, was nicknamed the "flying bar" because of the large quantities of vodka that were always carried in its hold.

While there were some discreet rest homes, primarily reserved for members of the *nomenklatura,* not much effort was made to fight alcoholism. It wasn't until Gorbachev, the last secretary-general of the Communist Party, took power that the gravity of the problem was officially recognized. He was personally affected: his brother-in-law was a serious alcoholic.

During the decline of the Soviet regime, Gorbachev raised the price of vodka by increasing taxes on it. But this policy imposed from above had the effect of further increasing

the bootlegging of *samogon,* a rough, dangerous vodka that the Russians always manufactured in times of shortage or social problems, no matter what regime was in power.

In this sense, the fall of communism did not have much effect on the place of vodka in Russian society, especially since the drink helped people to bear the ups and downs of a particularly unstable economic situation. As one of the editors of Pravda pointed out to the new owners when they called him a drunk: "Since my salary is just enough to buy a bottle of vodka, what else do you expect me to do with it?"

THE MOSCOW STANDARD

The advent of a market economy in Russia did have the effect, however, of inspiring a new aggressiveness among vodka producers.

Most production is in the hands of a group

belonging to the state, with distilleries not only in Moscow but also in other cities like Saint Petersburg, Samara, Irkutsk, Kaliningrad, Kaluga, and Kursk. Vodka exports are handled by a national agency, Soïouzplodoimport, which manages a large number of brands and has signed distribution contracts with European and American companies. Not long ago, independent distillers like Dovgan also began to appear.

Now that Soviet protectionism has ended, Russian producers are confronted with competition on two fronts.

On the one hand, foreign producers are flooding the Russian market. The authorities estimated in 1994 that 60 percent of the spirits consumed in Russia were imported. And, in 1995, at least 140 foreign brands of vodka were on sale in Moscow.

On the other hand, in foreign markets, Russian vodkas have been supplanted by many producers claiming Russian origin–or at least a semblance of it. In many cases, they don't even have to make the pretense in order to attract customers (the Scandinavians provide one example).

The Russians had begun their offensive by affirming the particularity of their vodkas, especially the higher-quality ones. Made pri-

Any occasion serves as an excuse to drink vodka, whether it's a gathering of students or a marriage celebration near St. Paul's Cathedral in Moscow.

marily from rye, they benefit from the soft waters of the Moscow region, especially the water from the Mytishchi springs, located twenty kilometers from the capital. The producers stress the fact that this water is never distilled or boiled, but simply filtered, either naturally or through membranes. Distillation is done fairly slowly in stages to allow the maximum extraction of the raw materials' flavors. Finally, the Russians mix the alcohol with water to reach an alcohol concentration of forty degrees in weight. They claim that other vodka makers dilute their vodka with an equal amount of water.

This Muscovite standard of quality, called *moskovskaia ossobia,* or Muscovite special, is based on the work of Mendeleyev and has been described in a book by William Pokhlebkin, *A History of Vodka,* published in London in 1992.

It provides a basis for Russian producers' claim in their advertising campaigns that "only Russian vodka is real vodka." They insist that other vodkas do not attain the same level of quality and even contain impurities that are dangerous to the drinker's health. Russian ad campaigns criticize "false" vodkas from Belorussia, Ukraine, Western Europe, the

Czech Republic, and even China. One Chinese brand, Langow, is treated as a poison because it contains twenty times the amount of aldehydes, five hundred times the amount of empyromatic oils and ten times the amount of complex ethers than is called for by current standards.

The consumer is even cautioned against so-called false vodkas bearing the labels of popular Russian brands. A brochure explains that "it should be verified that the mark on the ground-glass stopper corresponds to that on the bottle's label. It should be verified that the glue is evenly distributed around the label, although hand-glued labels are all different. The code number should have between seven and ten digits. The ground-glass stopper on a factory-made bottle should not turn around its axis; it would have been rejected at the factory if it did.»

On foreign markets, Russian producers quickly understood the rules of competition, as is shown by the agreement concluded in 1995 with the British group IDV for the development of Soïouzplodoimport's leading brand, Stolichnaya. IDV already owns Smirnoff, the world's best-selling brand of vodka, but in 1994 it lost the distribution rights to Absolut on the American market, where it is highly successful. A little earlier, in 1991, Boris Smirnov, the great-grandson of the founder of the renowned Smirnoff brand, started producing vodka under his own name, with a red label and bearing the coat of arms of his grandfather. He even obtained the approval of the Russian licensing administration a few days before the Heublein group (a subsidiary of IDV) received approval for the Smirnoff brand, which it has owned since 1938 and distributes in nearly 140 countries. Smirnoff, which until then had only been distributed in stores reserved for foreigners, obviously had a great potential for growth in Russia. There followed a series of trials, thundering pronouncements to the press, offers of friendly arrangements that were later denounced as corrupt,

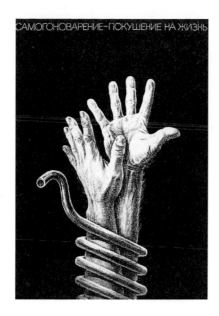

and so on. What was at stake in this battle, which mobilized many international lawyers, was not so much the domination of a market (Boris Smirnov hardly had the same means of production as the giant Smirnoff) as discovering whether Russia would accept international legislation on brand names or whether a brand like Smirnoff belonged to everyone in the end.

On average, each Russian drinks 14.5 liters of pure alcohol per year, or the equivalent of 170 half-liter bottles. Other alcoholic beverages are included, of course, but vodka takes the lion's share, making Russia one of the leading world markets. That is enough to whet plenty of commercial appetites and to increase the worries of Russian producers confronted with the ambitions of multinational competitors.

Russian posters for an anti-alcoholism campaign. The slogans say it all: below: "His outlook on the world"; right: "This isn't bravery, it's pure lunacy."

STYLES
AND BRANDS

The concept of a brand in Russia is not understood in the same way as it is in Western countries because of the long-standing manufacturing monopoly during the communist period. The names of the different vodkas produced in Russia refer more to different styles, and they may be made by several distilleries at the same time. In addition, these names are not attached to a particular family or region, but rather to certain qualities and flavorings. There is still a limited number of them, even though new brands and names have appeared since the collapse of communism.

Altai

Located in Russia, China, and Kazakhstan, Altai is a mountainous region (the name means "mountain of gold" in Mongolian), with an altitude of three thousand meters at its highest point. Vodka, made from varieties of wheat that are highly resistant to the low temperatures of this Siberian

With 8,000 lakes and 13,000 rivers, Altai is one of the most untouched regions in the world.

region, has been produced in the area for more than a century. The water there is especially pure.

This explains why the French group Pernod-Ricard decided to launch an international brand of vodka called Altai. Since 1994, the group had been looking for a high-range vodka that could compete with the leading brands.

Made in the village of Sokolovo, the vodka is made entirely of wheat, distilled three times and filtered several more. With an alcohol content of ninety-six percent when it comes out of the continuous still, it is then diluted with pure water from the Altai Mountains that surround the village. Packaged in transparent, silkscreened bottles, it has an alcohol content of forty percent.

In addition to a premium brand for the international market, the Pernod-Ricard group wanted to develop this vodka on the Russian market through the intermediary of its subsidiary Rouss. Even though it is one of the most expensive on the market, and one of the most recent, it was lauded in 1996 by the Izvestia newspaper as the "the best Russian vodka among those created since perestroika." As of 1998, this vodka will be distributed by Pernod-Richard subsidiaries in thirteen countries in Europe, Asia, and Australia.

Stolichnaya and Moskovskaya are the Cristall distillery's two leading brands.

Cristall

This high-range variety of Moskovskaya is made in Moscow in the city's main distillery, which also makes other vodkas. It is considered one of the finest for its subtle grain flavoring, but it is somewhat lacking in character because of its purity.

Dovgan

This new brand of Russian vodka appeared in 1996. It carries the name of Vladimir Dovgan, a businessman who is partly responsible for the opening of Russia to a market economy. In 1990, at the age of 26, he started manufacturing equipment and products for pizzerias and bakeries. He registered his name as a quality brand and label for different products.

To make a range of vodkas of high quality, he called on the top specialists in the field. As early as the first year of operation, the Dovgan range received awards at several fairs and expositions, not only in Russia (Moscow and Saint Petersburg), but also at SIAL in Paris and Anuga in Cologne. There are nine types of Dovgan vodka: Rye, Winter (flavored with mint), Cranberry, Lemon, Honey, Forest (St.-John's wort and forest herbs), Tzar and Gold (bay leaf and rose). They are sold in a variety of packages.

In 1997, Dovgan opened a production facility in Nimegue, Holland and then went after the European market with the help of a sales network. The company plans to go into business in the United States soon. Hoping to compete with premium vodkas by stressing its Russian origins, Dovgan is making its name known by sponsoring cultural and charitable events.

Left to right: Dovgan vodkas: Orange, Winter, Gold, for women, wheat-based.

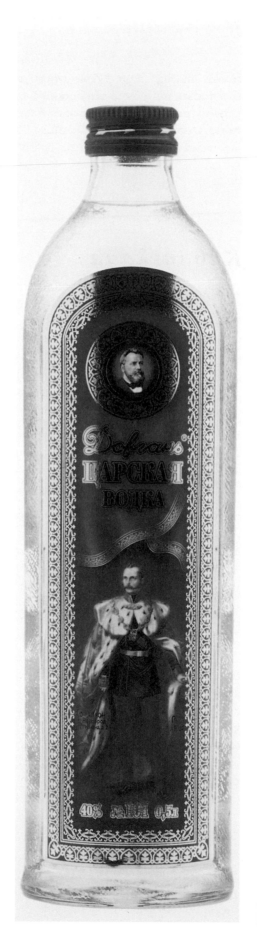

Krepkaya

In Russian, the word *krepkaya* means "strong," a good description for this vodka, with its alcohol content of fifty-six percent, making it one of the most alcoholic Russian vodkas. It nevertheless has real aromatic potential and a true personality, marked by distinctive spicy notes. Because of its strength, it can be either drunk straight or mixed in a cocktail.

Kubanskaya

This original vodka calls to mind the Cossacks of the Kuban River region, located in southern Russia, not far from Georgia. The vodka differs from the Moscow style in that it is distinguished by citrus (orange and lemon) notes that lend it a highly characteristic touch of bitterness.

Kremlyovskaya

Made in a new distillery located near Moscow, this vodka claims to be the vodka of the Kremlin. Distilled three times and filtered through charcoal, it contains 37.5 percent alcohol and also comes in versions flavored with lemon, pepper, and blackcurrant.

Limonnaya

Vodkas with lemon flavoring like this one are popular in Russia. Mild and unctuous (a little sugar is usually added to reduce the acidity of the lemon), it can be made in different ways. The most interesting versions are flavored with an infusion of lemon peel, while others simply have flavored concentrates added to them.

Left to right: Dovgan Lemon, Tzar, Forest, Honey, and Imperial (available as a gift only), and Kubanskaya vodka.

Moskovskaya

Named after the Russian capital city, this is the best example of the classic Moscow style of rye-based vodka (malted or non-malted), with no added flavorings and containing forty percent alcohol, in conformance with the principles of Mendeleyev. The Osobaya ("special" in Russian) version is in theory reserved for export and is a lemon-flavored beverage.

Okhotnichya

This is a flavored vodka that was the favorite of the hunters of yesteryear and anyone else who had to face the frigid Russian winters. It comes in many styles, depending on the brand and the producer. In the classic recipe, an infusion is prepared that contains around ten herbs and spices, including ginger, cloves, juniper, anise, and orange peel. This is added to a classic vodka made from grain, along with a little sugar and white wine, making it somewhat like port. The mixture is left to macerate for a while before it is distilled again and then bottled. It can contain up to forty-five percent alcohol.

Pertsovka

Peter the Great had the habit of sprinkling his glass of vodka with finely ground black pepper. Today, pepper vodka is made by macerating different types of chilies and peppers in grain-based vodka. The flavor is powerful and spicy, although the alcohol content is moderate (thirty-five percent). It is reddish-amber in color and facilitates the making of a Bloody Mary. There are many types of pepper vodka, depending on the producer and the market for which it is destined.

Left to right: Bravo-Bis, "One more glass!", "Warning from the police: If you've been drinking, don't drive!", "Little Birch" Russian vodka, Souvarov vodka.

Priviet

This vodka of Russian origin is mostly available in North America. Traditionally made of grains, it is distinguished mainly by its affordable market price.

Pshenichnaya

This vodka of highly satisfactory quality is unusual in that it is made exclusively of wheat. It has a mild flavor and contains forty percent alcohol.

Russkaya

This is one of the rare vodkas that dares to admit that it is partly made with potatoes. It is slightly flavored with cinnamon and contains forty percent alcohol. It exists in several versions characterized by great aromatic mildness.

Sibirskaya

Siberia, evocative of freezing cold, also stands for extreme purity, making it an excellent promotional device for this type of vodka, made with wheat flour and filtered several times through birch wood charcoal from the taiga. When tasted, it reveals pleasant aromas of anise. This vodka can be fairly strong; one version contains forty-two percent alcohol.

Smirnoff Black

In the 1980s, Smirnoff made a noted comeback in the city where it had been born more than a century before. To celebrate the event, the company chose to re-create the recipe of its founder, Piotr Smirnov. Made only of grains (with a high proportion of rye), Smirnoff Black owes its special characteris-

Left to right: Orpheus vodka (Saratov Province), banker's vodka, division commander's vodka, special Evridika vodka, the wise man of Yaroslavi's vodka.

tics to the use of an old-style pot still (the type used in Charente), which is better able to develop the aromas of the grain, and slow filtration through charcoal. Smooth and especially aromatic, it is an excellent tasting vodka.

Starka

Light amber in color and fairly aromatic, this is an "old" (*starka* in Russian) vodka. It is one of the rare vodkas that is, in principle, aged for a certain length of time. But its characteristics are due more to its aromatization by an infusion of apple- and pear-tree leaves, followed by another distillation with the addition of an *eau-de-vie* made from wine and a little port. It is very mild tasting in spite of its high alcohol content of at least forty-three percent.

Stolichnaya

A high-range Russian vodka that, is a perfect expression of the Moscow style. Its name means "capital" (*stolitsa* in Russian). Made from winter wheat, it is distilled twice and filtered through birch-wood charcoal three times. The water used to rectify it is both soft and pure. A little sugar is added at the end to make it smoother.

Left to right: special rye vodka, Generalissimo vodka, Ambassador vodka, the king's vodka, Stolichnaya vodka.

45

While its label still shows the facade of the Moscow Hotel, built under Stalin in the 1930s, Stolichnaya is now the leader of Soïouzplodoimport's exports. It is meant to compete with major international brands like Smirnoff and Absolut. A special effort is currently being made to conquer the American market through the intermediary of the importer Carillon. There are no fewer than ten varieties of Stolichnaya, in addition to the classic style, which comes in two strengths, with forty percent and fifty percent alcohol.

Made with natural flavorings, it comes in the following varieties: Ohranj (orange), Limonnaya (lemon zest), Pertsovka (pepper and chili), Okhotnichaya (herbs and spices), Kaffya (coffee), Vanil (vanilla), Strasberi (strawberry), Razberi (raspberry), Persik (peach), and Zinamon (cinnamon). Eight different varieties of Stolichnaya come in refrigerated bottles that bring it to the perfect serving temperature (minus one degree Celsius).

Stolovaya

With a fifty percent alcohol content, this is one of the strongest vodkas. It is usually drunk in small quantities with traditional meals. It is transparent and made exclusively of grains.

Ultra

This new Russian vodka, with its modern design and deep blue bottle, symbolizes the new face of today's Russia–no czarist or Stalinist symbols are associated with it. With an alcohol content of 37.5 percent, this is a grain-based vodka of great purity made with water from Lake Ladoga, the largest in Europe.

*Left to right: Ultra vodka, *XXX* vodka, Topaz vodka, Kolecnik (cartwright's) vodka, Governor of Golitsi's vodka.*

Zubrovka

Like its Polish cousin of the same

name, this traditional vodka is flavored with "buffalo grass," which grows in a region that extends into both countries. The Russian version, however, does not have a blade of grass in the bottle. Mild and smooth, with refined flavors, it contains forty percent alcohol and is a perfect accompaniment to traditional Russian cuisine.

Other varieties

There are several other brands of Russian vodka that are not as well-distributed as those mentioned above, including the relatively new Posolskaya, similar to the Moscow style; Stolbovaya, a grain-based vodka that also exists in pepper and anise versions; Yubileynaya, flavored with honey and brandy; Zolotoe Koltso; Anisovaya, flavored with anise; Baikalskaya, which reflects the purity of the waters of Lake Baikal; Maccahapa Zarskaya Datscha, in memory of Czar Nicholas II; Saint Petersburg; Star of Russia; Strovia; Viktoria; etc.

Left to right: Troika Siberian vodka, Istok vodka, special Kaloujskaia vodka, golden dome vodka, Tchaïkovski vodka.

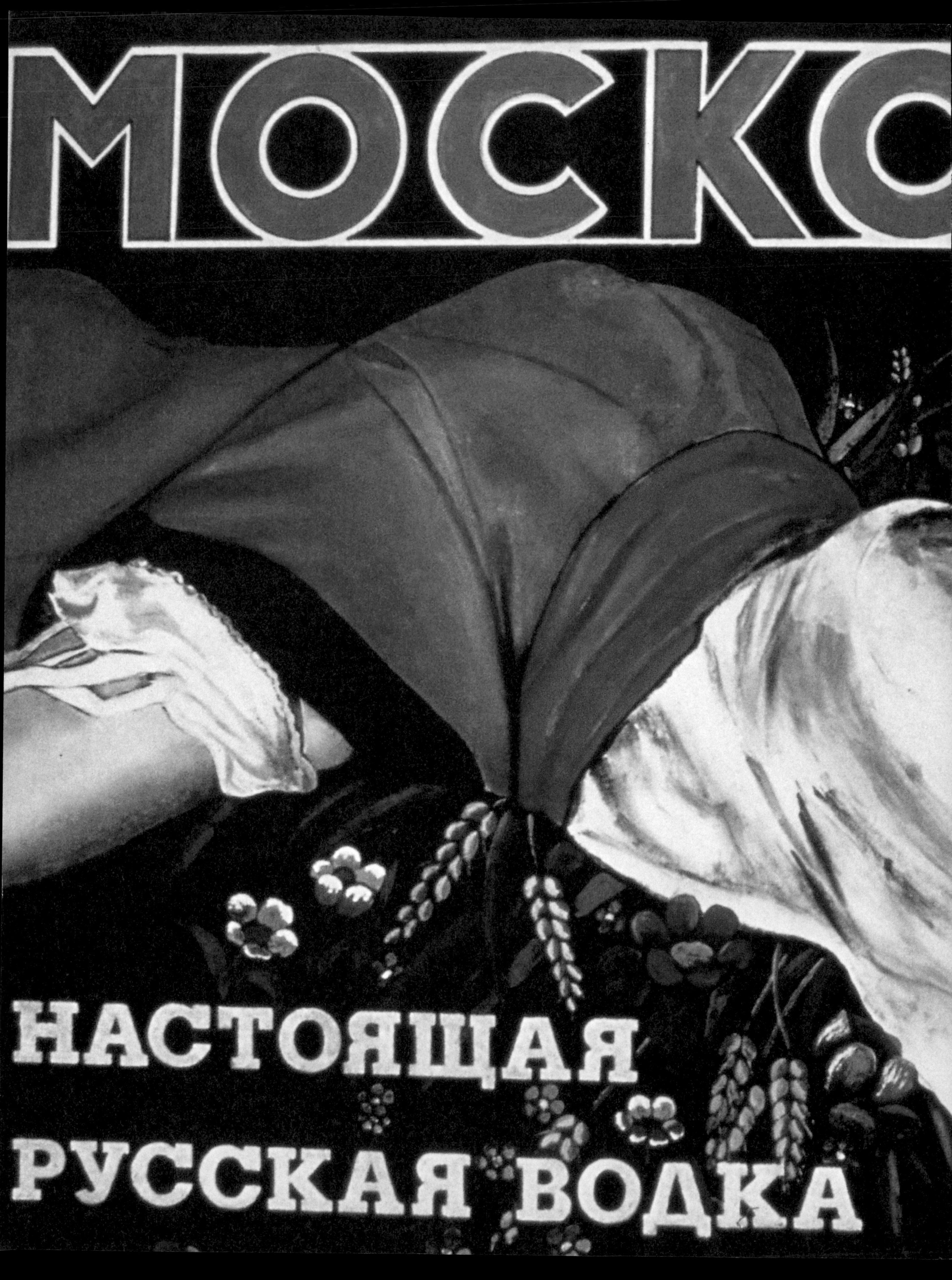
МОСКО
НАСТОЯЩАЯ
РУССКАЯ ВОДКА

SMIRNOFF: UP AND DOWN IN HISTORY

Smirnoff is the world's best-selling vodka and the second most popular brand of alcohol after Bacardi rum. The company has had an eventful history, passing from glory to oblivion and back again, punctuated by familial misunderstandings, a stint underground, expatriation, renewal, and a return to its origins.

It all began in Moscow in the early nineteenth century, around 1816. Two brothers, Yakov and Arseny Alexeyevich, arrived in the capital with their younger brother, Ivan, to set up a wine trading house and spirit manufacture. After the Napoleonic wars, the capital was booming. The two brothers were not yet officially called Smirnov because they were serfs and were dependent on their lord. That didn't stop them, however, from building up their company and making their fortune in the years that followed. In 1840, Ivan earned enough money to free himself from servitude and began to legally use the name Smirnov.

He opened his first establishment at 10 Barvarka Street in Moscow. At the same time, his brother Arseny was expanding his own business with the help of Yakov and, beginning in 1859, of his son Piotr Arsenyevich, who rapidly showed himself to be a true businessman. In 1862, Piotr took over the company's direction and created his own distillery. He was a much better salesman than his uncle Ivan, who was succeeded by his sons Sergei and Alexander. After competing with each other for a time, the two Smirnov companies finally merged in the 1880s

under the direction of Piotr, who was recognized as the head of the family.

The company established its reputation in part through the use of a new technique, charcoal filtration, which eliminated the maximum amount of impurities. According to the Smirnoff version of the story, it was one of the company's chemists, Andrey Albanov, who accidentally discovered the effectiveness of this technique during an experiment. He left a bottle of iodine tincture open all night near a piece of charcoal. The next morning, the charcoal was giving off a strong odor of iodine, demonstrating its powers of absorption. According to other sources, however, experiments had already been conducted on the use of charcoal as a filter for vodka as early as 1780 by another chemist, Theodore Lowitz, at the request of the czar. Other countries, including Poland and Sweden, also claim to have invented the technique.

Piotr Smirnov's business grew rapidly, both in Russia and abroad, thanks to the high quality of the vodka he produced and his good business sense. He became the official supplier of the Imperial Court in 1886, but in 1876 he was already participating in the Philadelphia Commercial Exhibition in the United States, which helped him to obtain the right to use an official coat of arms on his bottles the following year. He obtained three others, in 1882, 1894, and 1896, and they are still used on Smirnoff bottles today. In 1896, the P.A. Smirnov company was at the height of its glory. At the Nizhni-Novgorod Fair, its pavilion was a major attraction, with a live bear and waiters dressed in bearskins serving samples of vodka. Czar Alexander II made a well-publicized visit to the fair, and Smirnov became the sole supplier of Grand Duke Sergei Alexandrovich. The company's pre-eminence continued during the reign of the last czar, Nicholas II.

When he died in 1898, Piotr Smirnov left his five sons a fortune consisting of a company with more than 1,500

Facing page, top: The Smirnov range; bottom: Piotr Arsenyevitch Smirnov. Above: The Smirnov pavilion at the Nizhni Novgorod fair. Left: Bottles dating from before the 1917 Revolution.

employees that produced up to four million cases of vodka and other spirits. It was one of the wealthiest companies in the country.

NATIONALIZATION AND EXPATRIATION

While the company prospered, the seeds of discontent were being sown among Piotr Smirnov's sons. Some of them left the business and sold their shares. In 1910, the company's direction was taken over by Eugenia, the widow of one of the sons, but she left the company to live abroad and settled in Italy after remarrying.

Following the revolution in 1917, the company was quickly nationalized and

HOW I BOUGHT SMIRNOFF
BY JOHN MARTIN

We had been acting as Smirnoff's distribution agent for several years when, in 1939, the Smirnoff company went bankrupt, and Kunett tried to sell it. Finally, he came to me and offered me the company for $50,000. I turned him down. First, the business wasn't worth $50,000, and, second, Heublein didn't have $50,000 to spare. In the end, Kunett sold the business for the value of the used equipment, but I immediately understood that the only way to handle Smirnoff vodka was to obtain the distribution rights.

Rudolph Kunett and John Martin of Heublein.

its premises transformed into a state garage.

Vladimir Petrovich, one of Piotr's five sons, managed to flee the country, taking with him some money and the secrets of vodka-making that had made his family's fortune. Nicholas, Piotr's oldest son, passed on to him the right to represent the family.

Vladimir's lengthy wanderings took him to Poland and Turkey before he finally settled in France in 1928, first in Courbevoie, near Paris, then in Nice,

where he set up a distillery the following year.

It was at this time that Smirnoff was adopted as the spelling of the family name in the West. Vladimir, in spite of all his efforts (he even opened another distillery in Poland), never succeeded in reviving the business.

In 1933, he sold the company and its secret techniques to Rudolph Kunett (formerly Kukhesh), a businessman who worked for Helena Rubenstein. Once an alcohol supplier to Smirnov, he knew the vodka business well and planned to expand the Smirnoff company in North America, where Prohi-

bition had finally ended. Kunett set up business in Bethel, Connecticut, and began to produce vodka. But, once again, success was elusive. During the first year, Kunett sold only 1,200 cases of vodka, and 5,000 cases in 1937. It was not even enough to allow him to pay the fee for his distributor's license.

In 1938, Kunett sold his rights to the Smirnoff name and his distillery to John Martin, who owned a small spirits company called Heublein. Martin, who also lived in Connecticut, knew nothing about vodka; he was just helping out a friend. In 1941, Smirnoff sold more than 22,000 cases of vodka. It

was a substantial increase, but not enough to convince the directors of Heublein that the company had a real future. Then, with the entry of the United States into World War II, vodka production was stopped, along with that of many other spirits.

‡ET A FEW MUGS TOGETHER AND GIVE A SMIRNOFF

When it comes to entertaining, this is the drink that is. For a cool, refreshing Mule made with Smirnoff and 7-Up, as a delicious tonic, pour six parts and stir with their crystal clear Smirnoff, filtered through 14,000 lbs. of activated charcoal. Then try your own with the flavor of 7-Up. So never forget the rule for the Mule. Make it with ....

Always ask for *Smirnoff* It leaves you breathless

THE AMERICAN RESURRECTION

Ed Smith, a Smirnoff dealer in South Carolina, had considerably increased his sales by using a surprising advertising slogan that billed vodka as "White whiskey. No taste. No smell." It was enough to attract consumers who didn't like the strong aroma of whiskey and other spirits. And, most importantly, it meant that Smirnoff could be mixed with other ingredients without detracting from their flavors.

A cocktail based on Smirnoff had already been invented in 1941. The idea came from Jack Morgan, owner of a Los Angeles restaurant called the Cock 'n' Bull. He couldn't sell his stock of ginger beer, whose taste didn't appeal to American palettes, so he tried mixing it with Smirnoff and lemon juice. To promote Morgan's concoction, Martin had tankards engraved with the name "Moscow Mule" and decorated with a drawing of a kicking mule. It was a big hit in Manhattan bars.

After the war ended and production resumed, John Martin continued the promotion of Smirnoff with the help of the Moscow Mule. Using a brand-new

Many stars, including Woody Allen and Groucho Marx, lent their images to Smirnoff ad campaigns.

invention, the Polaroid camera, he took a picture of a bartender holding a bottle of Smirnoff and a Moscow Mule tankard. He then showed the photo to another bartender to prove to him that the cocktail was fashionable in his competitors' bars and that it was in his interest to promote it. He took a second photo and went to see another bartender, and so on. He always left a copy of the photo with the bartender so he could hang it in a prominent place in the bar to show off his fame to his customers.

From then on, the Smirnoff craze took off. The volume sales tripled between 1947 and 1950, and doubled again in 1951.

This was the height of the Cold War, and the promotion of a product of Russian origin was enough to shock more than one American. But John Martin

was able to turn even this problem to his advantage. He flaunted the Russian origins of Smirnoff and its czarist connections by putting the imperial emblems on the label. To drink Smirnoff was to take revenge on the Bolsheviks.

But more than anything else, Smirnoff's success in America was due to the neutral taste of the vodka, which allowed it to be mixed with any other ingredient. Ed Smith's slogan: "No taste. No smell." was abandoned because it was too negative and was replaced by another: "It leaves you breathless.»

This slogan was created during a reception given on Long Island. John Martin was serving cocktails made with Smirnoff, and one of the guests exclaimed: "It knocked me breathless." The advertising man Milton Goodman persuaded John Martin to make it the theme of his campaign. The slogan first appeared in an ad published in *Life* magazine in 1952. Used in a variety of different ways, the world "breathless" remained the favored slogan of Smirnoff for many years.

After the Moscow Mule helped Smirnoff sales take off, John Martin invented other cocktails in order to create more occasions for drinking vodka. Their exact origin is not always known, but Heublein was always able

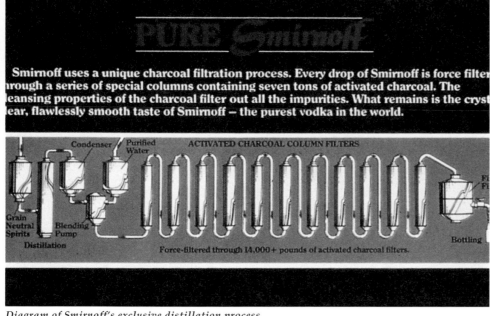

Smirnoff uses a unique charcoal filtration process. Every drop of Smirnoff is force filter[ed] [th]rough a series of special columns containing seven tons of activated charcoal. The [cl]eansing properties of the charcoal filter out all the impurities. What remains is the cryst[al] [cl]ear, flawlessly smooth taste of Smirnoff — the purest vodka in the world.

Diagram of Smirnoff's exclusive distillation process.

to use them effectively in the promotion of Smirnoff vodka.

One of the most famous of these cocktails, the Bloody Mary, had been created in 1921 by the bartender at Harry's Bar in Paris, Fernand Petiot, who called it "Bucket of Blood." When he moved to New York in 1934 and was working at the King Cole bar in Manhattan's Saint Regis Hotel, he changed the composition of the drink, adding spices and Worcester sauce to the tomato juice, and dubbed it a "Red Snapper." It was only later that the drink came to be called a "Bloody Mary."

Another famous cocktail of the 1950s was the Screwdriver (vodka and orange juice). It was named by American mechanics working in the Middle East, who mixed the drink with a screwdriver. The origins of other well-known concoctions like the Bullshot (vodka and beef bouillon) and the Black Russian (vodka and Kalhua, a coffee liqueur) are unknown, but they were probably invented by creative bartenders and later promoted by Heublein.

With his profits, John Martin was able to finance major advertising campaigns that were notable for their somewhat anticonformist stance. For

Americans, vodka was not a traditional drink that they were accustomed to but something new. Its neutral taste was unlikely to displease anyone, and drinking a vodka cocktail made the drinker seem fashionable and even ahead of the times. One of the advertising campaigns used the slogan "driest of the dry," illustrated by desert scenes that were superbly photographed in a surrealistic style by Bert Stern in Egypt, the Mojave Desert, and other places that were considered exotic by American consumers.

In another ad campaign, Heublein called on show-biz celebrities to appear in humorous situations while drinking a Smirnoff cocktail as a way of illustrating the drink's originality. Among the

Rudolph Kunett

stars who passed in front of the camera were Woody Allen, Groucho and Harpo Marx, Zsa Zsa Gabor, Buster Keaton, Marcel Marceau, Benny Goodman, Joan Fontaine, Vincent Price, and many others.

SMIRNOFF CONQUERS THE WORLD

By the end of the 1950s, Smirnoff had become an important brand name on the American market, and John Martin was already planning the company's international expansion. He sent Rudolph Kunett, who had owned the company in the 1930s, off to find

Tatiana Smirnov, the widow and heir of Vladimir, and to buy the worldwide rights from the Polish company.

In 1952, Heublein concluded a licensing agreement with the British company Gilbey for the production and sale of Smirnoff vodka in Britain, Canada, Australia, New Zealand, and South Africa. On the British market, an advertising campaign was quickly created that stressed the unconventional personality of the Smirnoff lover, who was portrayed as individualistic,

Above: Construction of the Smirnov factory. Below: Boris Smirnov.

relaxed, rebellious, and mysterious. The slogan: "The effect is shattering." Two years later, Heublein bought out the French branch of Smirnoff. This was the last of those founded by Smirnov family members, and Heublein was now assured of worldwide rights to the name. Licensing agreements were signed in Mexico, Spain, and Italy. By 1965, Smirnoff was exported to or manufactured under license in more than a hundred countries.

An international advertising campaign was born, using the slogan "Pure Thrill," and was used in all markets. Even James Bond participated, replacing his gin cocktails with Vodkatinis made with Smirnoff, designed to compete with dry martinis on the American market. Three years later,

Smirnoff was the number-one best-seller among spirits in the United States. The top spot was later lost to Bacardi throughout the world. Since then, Smirnoff has remained in second place, with sales of more than 170 million bottles.

The most popular vodka in the range is No. 21, with its famous red-labeled bottle. "Smirnovskaya Vodka N. 21" is written on the label in Cyrillic script in reference to the vodka Piotr Smirnov made for the czar's

armies. The grains it is made from are distilled twice in a process that takes twenty-four hours, then the liquid is filtered through charcoal made exclusively of hard woods. Pure water is then added to bring the degree of alcohol to 37.5 percent.

There are other, less well-known varieties that have a higher alcohol content. The Smirnoff with the silver label contains 45.2 percent alcohol and the one with the blue label has 50 percent alcohol.

THE RETURN TO RUSSIA

At around the same time that the Heublein company was being bought out by British International Distillers and Vintners (IDV) in 1987, Smirnoff made a triumphant return to Moscow and opened a distillery there.

Smirnoff Black is manufactured in Moscow with the same techniques used by Piotr more than a century earlier. It is made with high-quality Russian grains, and the mash is distilled in a copper pot still, creating a more aromatic vodka that is drunk straight and well-chilled or on ice.

The fall of the communist regime, however, was also a wake-up call to the sixty remaining members of the Smirnov family still living in Russia. One of them, Boris, Piotr's great-grandson, took the owners of Smirnoff vodka to court in an effort to have his family rights to the operation recognized. The first suit was thrown out of court, but another was initiated in 1996.

POLAND: AUTHENTICITY AND DIVERSITY

Along with its powerful neighbor, Russia, Poland is the "other" vodka-producing country, where vodka holds just as important a place in the history, culture, and daily life of the people. This is a country with a troubled history; it has been mistreated and even dismantled several times by the powers that surround it, including Russia, Prussia, and Austria. Yet Poland has been able to preserve its identity through its language, its Catholicism–and its vodkas. And, while the damage caused by many wars and occupations regularly led to the destruction of the country's distilleries, they were always reconstructed and the ancestral recipes preserved.

Of all the vodka-producing countries, including Russia, Poland doubtlessly offers the widest diversity of vodka styles. Today, there are more than one thousand different brands and varieties, a result of the Polish producers' ability to maintain and even rediscover traditional methods, but also because they were always willing to innovate and make use of the latest techniques and trends. This explains why vodka lovers can always count on making interesting new discoveries in Poland. They will not be disappointed.

Left: The last remaining European buffaloes on the Bialowesia reserve.
Above: Belvedere Palace, the presidential residence in Warsaw.

Until the eighteenth century, rye was the principal raw material used for making vodka in Poland.

In Polish, as in Russian, the word "vodka" is a diminutive of *woda* (the "w" is pronounced like a "v"), meaning "water," or a sort of concentrated water. The word has been used in Poland for many centuries, perhaps even since the eighth century, and throughout the Middle Ages, but it was mostly applied to medicinal preparations, or what might be called elixirs. The art of distillation was not yet known, and the alcohol content was low–around sixteen percent. These recipes, passed on mostly by monks, were used primarily to preserve plants and spices, with the goal of magnifying their therapeutic properties.

Sometime in the sixteenth century, spirits that were distilled at least twice began to appear in Poland. They were called *gorzalka,* a contraction of *gorzale vino,* which meant "burnt wine," and were made with the same techniques used in the production of the first spirits in the Netherlands. At the time, Poland had access to wines made in the south of the country, mostly from the Kraków region, for use in this new method. The beverage was also known as *okovita,* from the Latin *aqua vitae,* or "water of life.»

Grains, especially rye, had been used for some time in Poland to make beer, and its producers probably came up with the idea of distilling it, as the Dutch had done with wine.

Although there is a text dated 1405 and written in Polish that mentions the word "vodka," the name could not refer to a strong alcoholic beverage because the production technique was not known at the time. That does not stop Poland, however, from claiming to be the country that invented vodka–a way of affirming its pre-eminence over Russia.

This quarrel makes little sense in the historical context and serves mainly to fuel current national rivalries. What is certain is that the discovery of double distillation spread throughout Northern Europe in the space of a few decades at the end of the fifteenth century and the beginning of the sixteenth, at the same time that what were once medicinal preparations were transformed into beverages for everyday consumption.

Both vodka and *gorzalka* were at first used as medicines taken internally or as unguents for external use. They were also used as perfumes, cosmetics, and even as aftershaves. The tradition of making these preparations from all kinds of plants and spices continued in Poland for centuries, providing it with a national heritage and unequaled expertise, and explaining the great diversity and quality of today's Polish vodkas.

In a 1534 treatise, the herbalist Stefan Falimiz listed seventy-two different types of herb vodkas with a wide variety of uses. These preparations were an important component of the home pharmacy. They were stored in a locked chest whose key was kept by the mistress of the house. In the richer families, one of the maids was the guardian of the chest.

Vodka, *gorzalka,* and *okovita* coexisted in the Polish language at least until the end of the seventeenth century, before "vodka" won out definitively. This is how the Frisian Verdun described the Poles in 1672: "They especially appreciate the taste of vodka, which they call *gorzalka* in Polish and *crematum* in Latin. Even the most important aristocrats carry it in little boxes so they can drink it at any time.»

RAPID GROWTH

Beginning in the sixteenth century, the distillation of spirits, mainly from grains, grew rapidly. At first, the authorities encouraged the practice. A royal edict of 1546 authorized all Polish people to make their own spirits. Soon there were distilleries everywhere, especially in Kraków (the capital of Poland at the time), Gdansk, and Poznan. This liberalism did not last long, however; in 1572, the king gave a few nobles monopoly rights over distillation in exchange for tax revenues. In addition, the consumption of vodka was limited to those taverns that belonged to the aristocracy. This did not, however, impede growth: in 1580, there were forty-nine stills in the city of Poznan alone.

In 1595, Reverend Prowodowski noted that "breweries and distilleries have been built everywhere, and they consume not only all the grain available, but also whole villages." A historian, Mariusz Wolanski, recounts that "the artisans of Poznan reimburse their debts to the merchants of Wroclaw with vodka. For

example, a cobbler in Poznan, Fryderyck Szolc, had to reimburse in vodka a debt of 290 florins that he owed to Tomasz Gröer, a Wroclaw merchant.»

The great estates and many farms were equipped with stills of varying quality that produced enough alcohol for the family and its servants.

Faced with such growth, royals and aristocrats, the only ones in a position to profit from vodka consumption, raised vodka taxes, which reached ten percent of the sales

Above: Krakighteenth century, rye was the principal raw material used for making vodka in Poland.
naya vodka.
n near St. Paul's Cathedral in Moscow.il the eighteenth that the techniqueThe arms of the Potocki family can be seen on the old bottle. The label on the bottle on the right carries the brand-new Lancut logo.

price in the seventeenth century. In the eighteenth century, vodka became an important element of trade in Poland. From the production centers, vodka was sent via the Gdansk port to Saint Petersburg, Denmark, and England, and by river to Austria. Silesian merchants carried it along the roads to Prussia, and documents show exports of Polish vodka to Moldavia, Hungary, and as far away as the Black Sea.

At the time, distillation techniques were improving, and vodka began to be distilled an increasing number of times to enhance its quality. Rye was the most common raw material, followed by wheat and occasionally plums. Potatoes were not com-

monly used until the eighteenth century. King John III Sobieski brought them back from Austria after his victory against the Turks during the battle of Vienna in 1683, but for several decades, potatoes remained a simple curiosity that were seldom used until German settlers were invited to take over underexploited estates by King Stanislaw II Poniatowski, who was also the elector of Saxony. They taught Polish peasants how to grow potatoes,

which became a popular raw material. Varieties were selected that were well-adapted to distillation because of their high starch content, but rye continued to dominate in the production of vodka.

Distillation was done in at least three stages. The results of the first were called *brantowka*, the second *prostka* (simple) and the third *okowita* (water of life). The *okawita*, whose degree of alcohol did not exceed seventy percent, was then diluted with water to obtain *prosta wodka* (simple vodka), also called *ordynaryjna* (ordinary), which contained thirty percent alcohol or less.

To improve its quality, the vodka was distilled again, most often with herbs, plants, or spices, to obtain *alembikowka*. This technique helped to mask imperfections, since filtering techniques were not yet known. The process was based on the knowledge gained from the making of medicinal potions in the Middle Ages. One of the oldest and most famous was *zlota woda,* the golden vodka made in Gdansk under the Goldwasser brand name. Made from a strong vodka flavored with anise, various herbs and spices, and sandalwood and roses, it was sweetened with sugar, and a few flakes of gold were even added. But there were also many counterfeit versions that imitated well-known varieties and were sold at lower prices.

To strengthen these vodkas, pepper, various herbs (some of which, notably "wolf berries," were poisonous), and even nitric acid and other dangerous substances were added to them. Overall, however, the quality of Polish vodkas was widely appreciated in a growing number of European countries, and commercial rivalries with Russia and other vodka-producing countries quickly intensified. Jean Pasek, a seventeenth-century Polish writer, said of Russian vodka that it was "of such mediocre quality that it would kill a goat forced to drink it.»

The end of the eighteenth century saw the creation of real industrial distilleries like that of J.A. Baczewski in Lvov (at the time located in Poland, now in Ukraine), now operated by the Polmos distillery of Starogard; the Lancut distillery, founded in 1784 by Princess Lubomirska, which still exists two centuries later; and the Warsaw distillery, created at the beginning of the nineteenth century by Leon Nowachowicz, which quickly became a leader in Polish vodka production.

INDUSTRIALIZATION AND MONOPOLY

In the nineteenth century, the new technique of continuous distillation was introduced, making possible the production of purer vodka at much lower prices. The first continuous still was installed in 1871 at the Starogard distillery, which had been founded twenty years earlier. The others quickly followed its example.

Polish distillers continued to make their traditional flavored vodkas, however, and, as competition among them increased, they expanded their product range, sometimes offering dozens of varieties or more, without counting other flavored spirits and liqueurs. The Kasprowicz distillery in Gniezno, for example, had a catalogue of more than eighty-eight different products, including vodkas and liqueurs, at the end of the nineteenth century.

After World War I, Poland once again became independent, after having been occupied for more than a century by Prussians, Russians, and Austrians. In 1919, the young republic created a state monopoly for the production and distribution of vodka, with the goal of re-establishing and maintaining the level of quality. A national company was created in Warsaw that had the exclusive right to produce rectified alcohol and "pure," unflavored vodka. Seventeen other distilleries retained the right to make flavored vodkas as long as they bought their supplies of pure vodka from the national company (this system was re-established after World War II, which had caused enormous destruction to the whole country, including the distilleries).

Wisent vodka, made by Lancut, is flavored with buffalo grass.

In 1973, the monopoly was reinforced when all the distilleries were combined into one entity, the Polmos group. The export of Polish brands was entrusted to the Agros group, which already handled other agricultural and food products. In the 1980s, economic problems in Poland reached the point where vodka, like many other food products, was rationed to residents. While stores for foreigners stocked the best of the country's production (to bring in much-needed foreign currency), the Poles had the right to only a half-bottle per month. Naturally, those who didn't drink but still received their ration exchanged it for other products.

Clandestine distilleries, which, as in Russia, had always existed to some extent, took off again on both farms and in city apartments. It is even said that the sales of the game "The Little Chemist," which included a rudimentary coil, boomed at the time, well beyond what could have been accounted for by young Poles' love for chemistry. After the democratic elections of 1989, which brought down the military dictatorship and marked the end of the socialist regime, the Polish spirits industry was reorganized.

Each of the Polmos group's twenty-five distilleries became an independent commercial entity, even though the state was still more or less the owner, along with the employees. The brands that already existed on the market could be produced by each of these distilleries without purchasing the rights, as long as the distillery's name was printed on the label, and they continued to be exported by the Agros group, which was privatized in 1993 and retained the related rights. At the time, however, each of the distilleries was allowed to create new brands and to manages its sales as desired, even for exports. This decision obviously involved the creation of many new brands, and there are now more than a thousand. In addition, new independent distilleries were created alongside those of the Polmos group. The competition was extremely tough since advertising for alcohol was practically prohibited, and taxes amounted to eighty percent of the sales price. From 1989 to 1995, however, the domestic market was closed to foreign vodkas to aid the revival of the Polish industry. As a result, the IDV group quickly concluded agreements with a Polish distillery so it could make Smirnoff vodka in the country.

The growing trend was toward the making of pure, transparent, unflavored vodkas because they were easier to produce. These products benefited from aggressive marketing, both in Poland and abroad. Today, they represent eighty percent of total production (around fifty million cases per year), against sixty-three percent ten years ago. Traditional vodkas are now seriously threatened, even though they are still produced with the same concern for quality.

With the country's regained independence, Polish distilleries are now asserting their identity, and many of them are backed up by years of experience.

LANCUT

Located in the south of Poland in the Kraków region, this small city dominated by an impressive castle is home to the oldest distillery still operating in Poland. Owned successively by several noble families, the estate was equipped with a distillery in 1784 by Duchess Lubomirska. One of her grandsons, Count Alfred Potocki, took possession in 1823 and undertook the production of vodka (especially varieties flavored with anise), using more modern equipment. His heirs continued his work and also became involved in sales through the opening of stores in Galicia, Austria, and Hungary. The distillery was completely rebuilt in 1911-12 by his grandson

Roman, but the war followed and caused major destruction. Then came nationalization and even further damage caused by the retreat of German troops and the advance of the Russian armies. In spite of these setbacks, a good part of the equipment, including the stills, was saved. In the following years, the equipment was regularly modernized, especially the bottling equipment, which reached a daily capacity of 200,000 bottles.

For Lancut, the return of independence meant the continuation of the production of some sixty existing brands (including the major national brands) and the creation of a dozen new products, including the brand Lancut, a transparent pure grain vodka; 2 1/2 Cross, made according to one of Count Alfred Potocki's old recipes; the spicy, peppery CK Vodka; and Wisent, flavored with buffalo grass.

Its long history makes Lancut an interesting place to visit. A distillery museum displays old-fashioned equipment, with explanations of the style and techiques of Lancut vodkas. The museum in the castle where the noble families once lived is also worth a visit.

KASPROWICZ

Kasprowicz has been operating in the small city of Gniezno, east of Poznan (the capital of

The western facade of Lancut's château.

Alfred Potocki founded the Lancut distillery during the Industrial Age, and today the company takes pride in its use of the very latest rectifying and purification techniques and in a production capacity of approximately 200,000 bottles per day.

Poland at the beginning of the Middle Ages), for more than a century. At the end of the nineteenth century, the distillery had a range of nearly one hundred spirits and liqueurs. It owes it fame to Gnesnania Boonekamp, a vodka-based liqueur flavored with twenty-three different herbs and spices.

POZNAN

Located near Lake Malta, Polmos Distilleries of Poznan (Poznanskie Zaklady Przemyslu Spirytusowego) has been operating for more than seventy years, but the region's vodka production is much older, going back to at least the sixteenth century.

Since the institution of the state monopoly in 1919, the main role of the Poznan distilleries has been to make rectified *eaux-de-vie* for other producers. The distilleries have high-performance, highly automated modern equipment and employ around 700 workers.

While it produces some major brands, including Wyborowa, Polonaise, and Krakus, the enterprise also has its own brands, including traditional ones like Kasprowicz, Hartwig-Kantorowicz, and Strzelczyk, and the more recent ones that are allowed by the new system in Poland. Most are transparent vodkas of great purity, like Premium, which is distilled several times and contains forty percent alcohol; Posnanian, also containing forty percent alcohol, which is made with an older technology to reproduce its traditional flavor; and Lodowa, which means "ice" in Polish.

In all, the Poznan Distilleries currently make more than sixty-five different vodkas and other spirits, many of which have received numerous awards both in Poland and abroad.

ZIELONA GORA

Grapevines once grew in this region in the west of Poland, not far from the German border, which explains the long-standing presence of distilleries there. LWWG, one of the Polmos group's distilleries and a descendant of other installations dating back to 1860, has been in Zielona Gora for more than fifty years. Equipped with ultramodern equipment, it makes not only the best-known vodkas in

Poland today (Wyborowa and Zubrowka), but also a range of more than one hundred spirits and liqueurs of all types. Recent competition has led it to produce several new brands, including Wodka Krolewska ("royal vodka" in Polish), a vodka of great purity that is not lacking in character, presented in packaging adorned with the symbols of the former Polish kingdoms.

STYLES
AND BRANDS

Poland's prolific production of vodka is complicated by the fact that different distilleries can make the same brand, in addition to making their own version of a general style, and can also have their own brands, many of them created only recently. This makes it difficult to mention all the different Polish brands; many of them taste alike and have similar packaging and names.

Though faced with such diversity, the vodka lover can be reassured on one point: any vodka "made in Poland" is at least of satisfactory, if not excellent, quality.

To understand the labels, it is important to know that certain descriptions correspond to an increasing level of purity: *zwykly* (standard), *wyborowy* (superior), and *luksusowy* (luxury).

The Baltic

The plains bordering the Baltic Sea are an excellent potato-growing area, where the Poles have developed special high-starch varieties for vodka-making. After saccharification (the breaking down of the starches into simple sugars) and fermentation, the mash is distilled several times and rectified to eliminate any undesirable elements. This vodka with a forty-percent alcohol content nevertheless has mellow flavors that are characteristic of the raw material. The Baltic "Special" variety is improved by the addition of a little rye-based *eau-de-vie* that has been aged in casks.

Barowa

This is a new brand of pure-grain alcohol, made by the Poznan Distilleries, with an alcohol content of forty percent.

Bielska

Located near Slovakia, the city of Bielsko-Biala has long been renowned

for the quality of its *eaux-de-vie*, especially those made from plums *(slivovice)*. This new brand of grain-based vodka (with thirty-eight or forty percent alcohol) is lightly flavored with plant extracts.

Black Currant

This is a blackcurrant-flavored vodka make by the Zielona Gora distillery, with thirty percent alcohol.

Chopin

The name of one of Poland's most famous native sons is also that of a new brand of vodka created after the liberalization of 1991. Made from rye and presented in a superb silkscreened bottle, it is produced by the Polmos distillery of Siedlce.

Cytrynowka

This lemon-flavored vodka is made through a complex process, using the

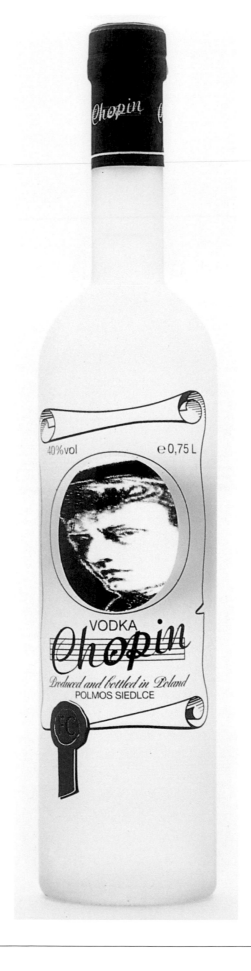

zest of the fruit and the leaves of the tree, all infused in a neutral vodka, then distilled again. As a result, the flavor of lemon is present without being invasive, creating a vodka of great finesse. It should be drunk on its own or with a dessert, since its slight acidity brings out the sweetness.

Czardasz

Its Hungarian-inspired name indicates that this is a vodka flavored with paprika, which gives it a slightly peppery taste.

Gnesnania Boonekamp

Flavored with twenty-three different herbs and spices, this rectified-alcohol-

based vodka is made by the Poznan Distilleries. A descendant of the first medicinal vodkas, it has an alcohol content of forty percent. While it makes a good aperitif because of its slight bitterness, this vodka, the distiller states, can also have a beneficial effect on the metabolism.

Hunter

This is the brand-name of a dry vodka flavored with juniper berries, with a little added sugar. Called Mysliwska in Polish, it has a forty-five percent alcohol content and is the traditional *eau-de-vie* of hunters.

Jarzebiak

This popular vodka with 40 percent alcohol is flavored with a liqueur made

In spite of the size of the Polish Jewish community before its extermination by the Nazis, kosher vodkas are a relatively recent invention, with the exception of an episodic history in Silesia, where the distillation of plum *eau-de-vie* is more common. The latest example comes from a man named Zygmunt Nissenbaum, a survivor of the Warsaw ghetto and the founder of a foundation that bears his name. In 1987, he began making a kosher vodka in partnership with Polmos. Its production is inspected yearly by rabbis, and the rules specify that the water used must come from an inhabited region and must not be used for agricultural purposes. The bottles must be sterilized before each use. The process has to be completely automated, without human intervention at any stage, from distillation to bottling. The equipment must be used only for this purpose.

Such rules raise production costs, but the brand has had a great deal of commercial success, both in Poland and on export markets, an indication of its quality. The Nissenbaum Foundation has set up its own distillery in Bielsko-Biala, with a range of grain- and potato-based vodkas (under the brand Nisskosher), as well as an herb-flavored version. They have been approved by the American Union of Orthodox Jewish Congregations. Profits are used for the renovation of Jewish cemeteries and monuments in Poland.

Inspired by the success of these kosher vodkas, other Polish distilleries have created their own: Bielsko-Biala's Happy; Zielona Gora's Koszerna; Poznan's Herzl; and Lancut's David, Rebeka and Judyta. Many of these vodkas are slightly flavored with a little fruit *eau-de-vie.*

from serviceberries, which are picked just after the first freeze, condensing their aromas.

The preparation is also enriched with aromatic extracts of figs, grapes, and prunes; sugar; and *eau-de-vie* made from wine. It is then barrel-aged for several months. The resulting vodka has great aromatic finesse, with slightly bitter notes. It makes an excellent after-dinner drink or a good base for cocktails. The "luxury" version contains forty-three percent alcohol. This is an example of the fine art of Polish distilling.

Karpatia

A small amount of fruit *eau-de-vie* is added to this new grain-based vodka, which contains between thirty-eight and forty-two percent alcohol.

Kasztelanska

This is one of the few vodkas that is aged in oak barrels, giving it an amber color. It has complex aromas, with nuances of spices and vanilla that show great finesse.

Krakus

The name refers to Kraków, the former capital of Poland. This high-quality vodka is made solely from rye, is distilled twice, and contains forty percent alcohol. Its appealing mellowness has made it a long-standing favorite.

Krolewska

A new brand launched by the Zielona Gora distillery, this top-of-the-range vodka has already had some success thanks to its aromatic purity, pleasant fruitiness, and a certain mellowness. It comes in a handsome bottle with a satiny surface, decorated with the arms of the royal Polish dynasties. There are two versions, with forty percent and forty-two percent alcohol.

Lanique

This is a range of flavored vodkas produced by the Lancut distillery in partnership with a British company. Among them are Cherry, Lemon, Plum and Pétale de Rose, a variety that was fashionable at the beginning of the twentieth century, described as "more precious than gold.»

Luksusowa

The word used for "luxury" vodkas is also the brand name of a potato-based vodka produced by the Poznan Distilleries. This mellow vodka comes in two versions, with forty percent and fifty percent alcohol.

Monopolowa

This pure-grain vodka is made according to an eighteenth-century recipe that was used by the Baczewski family of Lvov (which belonged at the time to Poland). It is now made by the Starogard distillery in Gdansk. It exists in a thirty-eight percent version (with a red cap) and a forty percent version (blue cap).

Pieprzowka

Made from grain and distilled twice, this vodka is flavored with various types of pepper and other aromatic elements. Spicy and strong (with forty-five percent alcohol), but not excessively so, it is the perfect accompaniment to traditional meals.

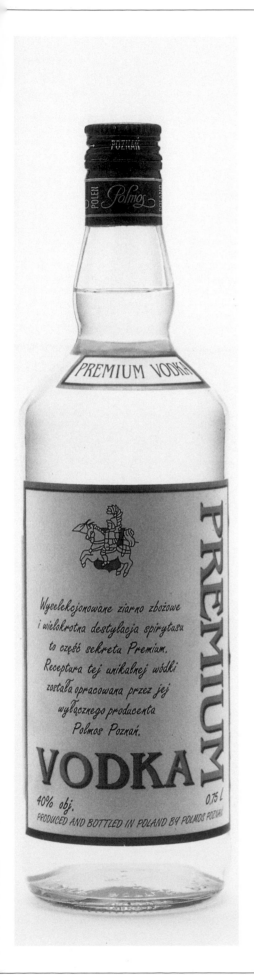

Polish Pure Spirit

As an example of its distilling prowess, Poland sells a line of perfectly rectified *eaux-de-vie*, Spirytus Rektyfikowany, containing fifty-seven percent, seventy-nine percent, and even ninety-five percent alcohol. Obviously, they are not meant to be drunk straight, especially the strongest one. Their perfect neutrality makes them a good base for all kinds of cocktails.

Polonaise

A fairly neutral vodka, this is one of the new brands launched by the Zielona Gora distillery since it became independent. Two types are available: White Label, with a forty percent alcohol content, and Blue Label, with fifty percent.

Premium

As its name indicates, this is a top-of-the-line vodka of great purity. Distilled four times, it has a certain mellowness.

The quality and modern packaging mark this vodka made by the Poznan Distilleries as an export product. It has a forty percent alcohol content and also comes in lemon- and pepper-flavored versions.

Soplica

Made according to an old recipe, this vodka is flavored with aged wine-based *eau-de-vie* and apple alcohol and macerated with dried fruits. Barrel-aging lends it a lovely amber color and full flavor. The name comes from a Lithuanian family of lords that figured in an epic poem, "Pan Tadeusz," written by the best-known Polish romantic poet, Adam Mickiewicz.

Starka

A highly traditional rye vodka, similar to the old Polish *gorzalka*. It is not rectified, but distilled in a pot still. After a little Malaga is added, it is aged at least ten years in small oak barrels. It contains between forty-three percent and fifty percent alcohol. Its woody flavor, marked with vanilla, is remarkable, as are its mellowness in the mouth and a certain sweetness. This is a vodka that should be served ice-cold.

Tatra

Named after the Tatra Mountains, which form the border with Slovakia, this vodka is flavored with various herbs, including angelica, giving it a fresh taste. With a forty-five percent alcohol content, it is drunk mostly in the summer with ice cubes and cold water.

Vistula

Made of potatoes grown on the banks of the Vistula, this vodka is distilled with a little malted barley, then rectified to eliminate unpleasant tastes. Its sweet aromas become stronger when it is shaken before being served.

Wisniowska

An interesting vodka flavored with cherries of a variety selected especially for this purpose.

Wyborowa

The name means "superior," and this pure-rye vodka is the best-selling Polish brand and the second in the world after Smirnoff. It is made with a special variety of rye grown in various regions of Poland, which give it a specific taste that is also due to double distillation, after each stage of which only the best alcohol is retained. The third step, which is kept secret by the distillers, gives Wyborowa its special character. The water used is especially soft and is filtered by inverse osmosis to purify it even further. The vodka's slight sweetness is not the result of the

addition of sugar as in other vodkas, but of the nature of the rye used to make it. Elegant and refined, it makes a perfect base for cocktails, especially with Dry Martini. When shaken, it goes equally well with caviar and smoked salmon. The brand dates to the 1920s, but its old-fashioned-looking label, which has now become chic, was designed in 1962. It is available in versions with 37.5 percent, 40 percent, 45 percent and 59 percent alcohol, and there are also varieties flavored with lemon, orange, pineapple, peaches, melon, and pepper, mostly for the North American market. Wyborowa is produced at several distilleries, and 6.7 million cases were sold in 1997.

Ziolowa Mocna

This potato-based vodka with forty-four percent alcohol is flavored with several herbs and has a very mellow taste.

Zoladkowa Gorzka

This vodka's dry, somewhat bitter taste comes from the herbs used to flavor it. With forty percent alcohol, it has an amber color and is recommended as a digestive aid.

Zubrowka

This famous vodka is distributed internationally and owes its reputation to its flavoring with buffalo grass, *hierochloe odorata* or *hierochloe australis* in Latin. This rare plant grows wild in the Bialowieza forest, in the east of Poland, where the last buffaloes in Europe run free (under the careful surveillance of man). It has a delicate, characteristic flavor and is harvested during a short period in the summer, at the hottest possible moment. It is then dried and used in the distillation of grain *eau-de-vie* (forty percent alcohol). A blade of the

grass is added during bottling just for decoration, distinguishing it from the Russian version, which uses no grass. Although the familiar figure of the buffalo and the vodka's supposed medicinal qualities are appreciated, this vodka should be cherished above all for its unique taste; it has a refined flavor of herbs, an amazing mellowness, and a strong and lingering taste. In *The Razor's Edge,* Somerset Maugham wrote that it is "so sweet on the palate and so pleasant that it is like listening to music in the moonlight.»

Zubrowka is mostly drunk straight, well-shaken, as an accompaniment to a number of traditional dishes from Poland or Northern Europe.

The success of this brand, made by several distilleries belonging to the Polmos group, has lately led to the appearance of other is flavored with buffalo grass, including Wisent and Turowka.

Zytnia

Often accompanied by the qualifier "Extra," this traditional rye vodka, flavored with a little apple or other fruit *eau-de-vie,* contains forty percent alcohol. Very popular in Poland, it has an obvious flavor of grains, with a certain sweetness in spite of its mostly dry taste. The "special" version, with forty-five percent alcohol, has an even stronger taste of rye.

SCANDINAVIA: PURITY MEETS PURITANISM

Located around the Baltic Sea, the Scandinavian and Baltic countries developed the art of distilling spirits from grains and potatoes at the same time as the rest of Northern Europe. In these countries, however, the term "vodka" is more restrictive than it is in Poland or Russia; it is mostly used to designate transparent spirits with little or no flavoring that are highly rectified, like the Swedish brand Absolut. Other types, made in a more traditional way, are usually called *brännvin* (burnt wine) or *akvavit (eau-de-vie)*. These different names are an expression of national identity, but the products themselves are very similar.

Highly appreciated in such rough climates, these spirits became extremely popular, and at one point most households had their own stills. A high level of alcohol consumption was encouraged by the low cost of the alcohol, leading to a puritanical reaction in the nineteenth century. State monopolies were set up for both production and importing, as well as for the distribution of alcoholic beverages, which was not the case in most other places. It wasn't until the end of the twentieth century that the countries on both sides of the Iron Curtain rediscovered a certain degree of freedom in terms of distilling, as in other domains.

Two examples of the splendor of the Finnish countryside: Lapland, land of the midnight sun (left), and the Pielinen Lake region (above).

Gamla Stam Island in Stockholm, a historical quarter of the Swedish capital.

SWEDEN

In Sweden, the first mention of spirits appeared in the fifteenth century with the use of the term *brännvin*, which etymologically means "burnt wine." These were mostly medicinal potions, probably with a low alcohol content, that were very costly because the wine had to be imported from more southerly countries. A document dating from the time explains that *brännvin* could cure at least forty different afflictions, including migraine headaches, lice, kidney stones, toothaches, and female sterility. Flavored or spiced versions were also know as *akvavit,* from the Latin aqua vitae, or "water of life.»

Curiously, *brännvin* was also used to produce cannon powder, as reported in an accounting ledger dating from 1467. The first known license for the production and distribution of alcohol was accorded in 1498 to a certain Corth Flaskedragare in exchange for providing the government with supplies to make cannon powder. But *brännvin's* use as a beverage had already began to spread, and the authorities were beginning to get nervous about it. Anyone caught selling *brännvin* for another use was subject to prosecution.

The Swedes, like all the natives of the Baltic nations, knew about the existence of "strong waters," brought to their countries by the Dutch and Germans of the Hanseatic League.

With the perfecting of the stills and the growing use of grains (much cheaper than wine) as a raw material, the distillation of spirits began to increase beginning in the seventeenth century.

At the time, especially during the reign of Gustav Adolph II (1611-1632), Sweden had attained a great level of power in Europe, dominating the entire Baltic region and fighting wars on Russian territory. It was perhaps during one of these military incursions that the term "vodka" was adopted. It was used only for transparent, unflavored spirits made of grain.

Even though it brought in increasing tax revenues to the state, the growth of *brännvin* also worried the authorities. In 1863, the governor of the northern province of Sweden wrote a report that "both soldiers and farmers are attracted by the drinking of *brännvin*, and are thus ruining their health and their well-being, neglecting both their work and their military service." A century later, the celebrated botanist Carl von Linné also took on *brännvin*, saying that it had "the same effect as the lash of a whip on a mare: It makes her react immediately, but does nothing to increase her strength.»

Nonetheless, by the middle of the eighteenth century, there was about one still for every ten inhabitants of Sweden. Every family and farm had its own for a good reason: while consumption in city cabarets was taxed, home production was still duty-free. The homemade alcohols varied greatly, and local languages had different terms for each type of spirit, according to the occasion on which it was drunk: while hunting, fishing, traveling, or even before going to bed.

At the same time that Protestant Puritanism was leaning toward increasing control over the daily lives of the people, a series of poor grain harvests led the authorities to ban home distilling in order to save the wheat and barley for foodstuffs. Around 180,000 stills were seized in the country in 1756. A state monopoly was set up for the production, sale, and import of spirits and other alcoholic beverages. Thirty official distilleries went into production.

Above, top, and left: The Vin&Sprit group was founded after World War I. For nearly eighty years, its status as a monopoly allowed it to corner the Swedish spirits market.

But, as elsewhere, these measures led to an increase in clandestine distilling, to the consternation of the authorities, who regularly reaffirmed the monopoly under pressure especially from the Swedish Temperance Society, founded in 1837 by Puritans. Home production was once again completely forbidden in 1860, but in the meantime, technological progress had already greatly reduced the number of stills being used, which dropped

from 173,000 in 1829 to 33,000 in 1853, and 564 in 1860. Improving methods allowed the making of spirits of better quality at a lower cost. The first continuous stills were installed near Stockholm by Lars Olsson Smith, the creator of the famous Absolut vodka (see the following chapter) in 1869.

The civil and religious authorities did not, however, give up the fight against alcoholism, which reached its

heights after World War I with the creation of Vin&Sprit. Production and sales of spirits were concentrated in this monopoly, the exclusive sales outlet for all alcohol. Heavy taxes hiked up prices and, for many years, consumers had ration books to keep track of their purchases of alcoholic beverages. Even American Prohibition did not go that far in the fight against alcoholism.

It was only when they left their country that the Swedes could easily consume alcohol, which perhaps explains the popularity of tours of Southern Europe after World War II.

In spite of all that, Vin&Sprit developed great *savoir-faire* when it came to distilling and made spirits of excellent quality. Some imitations of foreign beverages like brandy, cognac, or calvados were occasionally even judged superior to the originals during blind tastings.

THE END OF THE MONOPOLY

While Sweden remained neutral during the two world wars and spent decades constructing its unique welfare state, it could not remain isolated indefinitely. In 1995, the country joined the European Union.

Membership in this open economic system meant that the Vin&Sprit monopoly could no longer continue. The group, now subject to national and international competition, shut down its distribution subsidiary, Provinum, and concentrated on two companies: Vin&Sprit Norden for the production and distribution of foreign spirits and wines, and Absolut Compagny for the manufacture and sales of Swedish vodka.

The competition in distribution was felt immediately, especially for wine, and the net sales of this branch dropped by two-thirds between 1994 and 1996.

Vin&Sprit is still the main producer and distributor of spirits in Sweden. It is currently trying to reinvigorate the image of the strong brand names it represents.

Unspiced vodka and *brännvin* represent nearly sixty percent of the spirits produced by V&S Norden. Explorer, the leading brand sold in Sweden, contains thirty-eight percent alcohol, and its label is decorated with a superb drakkar. Absolut holds only third place, behind Renat *brännvin*, a brand created in 1877 that contains thirty-nine percent alcohol. There is also the very smooth Kron vodka, created in 1920; Nyköpings (flavored with anise); and Jägar *brännvin*. The company also makes a line of akuavits with different flavors (see the chapter devoted to them).

While still very recent, the end of the state monopoly has already led to the arrival of new operators on the Swedish market, not counting the foreign producers that now have more freedom to sell their spirits.

Founded in 1893, Saturnus, based in Malmö, is one example of a company ready to attack the market after having "waited a century to throw its punch." Its founder, Fritz Borg, was a pharmacist and started by making various liqueurs. When his company was forbidden to produce alcoholic beverages, it turned to the extraction of natural perfumes for both beverages (especially sodas) and other food products.

Over the years, it developed a high level of expertise (confirmed by the awarding of the ISO 9001 standard) that was just waiting for the fall of the V&S monopoly to be exploited. Saturnus quickly put on the market a range of several spirits, including Extra *brännvin;* various schnapps (*snaps* in Swedish), including Pasksnaps, Midsommar, Kräftsnaps, Julsnaps, and Punsch (made according to the founder's recipe); and a variety of liqueurs and aperitifs.

Svensk Vodka claims to be the first independent distillery, created in 1917. Its owner, Erik Lallerstedt, was until 1995 a well-known restaurateur in Stockholm and, as soon as the monopoly ended, began to market vodka. "Quality without compromise" is the motto of the company, which is based in Motala in the center of Sweden. This location was chosen because the family of his partner, Mikael Andersson, has been making spirits there for more than a century.

The product range is derived directly from this tradition, and the company seeks out old *brännvin* recipes that were used for cooking but were also drunk on their own. The packaging, however, is modern, and each variety is named after its degree of alcohol: 23, 32, 38, and 60, printed in large characters on the label. It's a simple but effective concept. The one called 23 is the result of a deliberate decision to create a high-quality drink with a low alcohol content.

Recently, Svensk Vodka put on the market a transparent *brännvin* in a bottle with a clean design, along with

vodkas under the Izy brand, flavored with peach and lemon.

The J&J Nordic company in Källby, founded in October 1995, took advantage of the end of the monopoly to begin importing and distributing wine, vinegar, and olive oil. Since October 1997, it has also been producing its own vodka, named Thors Hammer–after the Scandinavian god of thunder–to clearly indicate its Swedish origin. This vodka ranks among the best. It has an alcohol content of thirty-eight percent and is diluted with the melted waters of ancient glaciers that have been protected from pollution.

ABSOLUT:
VODKA AS A CONCEPT

The history of Absolut Vodka is doubtlessly one of the most fascinating in the long history of spirits. It serves as proof that, beyond the intrinsic qualities of the product, advertising and marketing are today the real masters of a brand's international success.

The birth of this vodka was marked by a strong Swedish personality, Lars Olsson Smith, born in Kiaby in 1836. It was said that he was already doing business at the age of ten. He started as a spirits broker and by the middle of the century controlled a third of the market, earning him the nickname *brännvins-kungen,* or king of *brännvin.* In this capacity, L.O. Smith quickly collided with the protectionist stance of the city of Stockholm, and rather than accept its regulations, he moved to an island, Reimersholme, located a few minutes away by boat but outside the municipal jurisdiction.

Waging a veritable commercial war, his company sold its spirits at a lower price than those in the city and even offered its customers a free round trip to the island. The affront to the city was such that Stockholm extended its territorial limits, but Smith only moved to another island a little farther away. Gunfire was even exchanged during this war of spirits.

L.O. Smith was also concerned about quality. He felt that the vodkas and *brännvins* of his time were not pure enough. When he discovered the existence of a new distilling method, rectification, he immediately started using it in his distillery. In the beginning, he used potatoes as a raw material. In 1879, he trademarked the name "Absolut Rent Brännvin," which translates as "absolutely pure vodka," for his new product.

He then went into business in the Skäne region in the south of Sweden, the country's wheat basket, and started using wheat flour instead of potatoes to make his vodkas. Once again, he drew attention to himself by waging war against the protectionist distribution system, accusing it of selling only spirits of poor quality. He even brought the unions into his boycott campaigns against stores accused of exploiting consumers. Then he turned toward exports and argued that his vodka was the purest in the world. Altogether, Smith won and lost three fortunes in his lifetime and he died debt-ridden in 1913. In 1906, however, his son had a modern distillery built in the city of Ahus in the south of Sweden. The company

Lars Olsson Smith

Above and facing page: Absolut vodka is distilled and bottled in the Limmared factory near Ahus, the bread basket of Sweden. Once packaged, the famous bottle, whose shape is copied from an antique medicine bottle, is sent out to conquer the world.

was finally nationalized in 1917 with the institution of the V&S monopoly.

THE CONQUEST OF AMERICA

Absolut remained little known for many years, and the directors of V&S, more bureaucrats than salespeople, did little to develop the company.

That all changed in the 1970s with the arrival of a real manager as the president of the group. Lars Lindmark's mission was to modernize the company and develop its exports, which had been neglected since the days of L.O. Smith. And, as the company knew little about modern sales techniques, he called on an outside consultant, Curt Nycander, to revamp Absolut's presentation and communications policy from top to bottom. The goal was to attack the American market, the largest vodka market at the time (imports were still banned in the USSR). Everything had to be ready for 1979, the hundredth anniversary of Absolut's trademark. That goal would eventually be reached, but in the meantime, many decisions had to be made. How should Absolut be defined, positioned, presented?

And, first of all, how should it be distributed? Lindmark and Nycander went to the United States in 1978 with their vodka samples,

including Absolut, to look for an American importer. They were not well-received. None of the major groups at the time–Hiram Walker, Seagram, Brown Forman, etc.–were interested in a vodka from Sweden, a country that was practically unknown to the Americans.

Finally, the Swedes were able to interest a small importer, Carillon, whose means were much more modest than those of the larger companies. Its entire management team consisted of the owner, Al Singer, and his sales director, the Frenchman Michel Roux. They distributed the French liqueur Grand Marnier and the English gin Bombay, along with a few European wines, in the United States.

The resulting combination of highly diverse talents relied more on luck than know-how. To define the shape of the bottle, the best Swedish designers were called in, but the results were not satisfactory: a jug in the shape of a Viking, an old-style flask, a black bottle bearing the arms of the Swedish royal family, and so on.

The directors of V&S then went back to the original concept of Lars Olsson Smith: the absolute purity of the vodka. Then, by chance, Gunnar Broman, one of the Swedish advertising men, discovered in an antique store an old medicine bottle with a wider-than-usual neck.

Everyone concerned was quickly convinced once it was decided that an innovative approach would be taken and pushed to its limits: The bottle would be perfectly transpa-

would win over consumers. Once again, luck played a role.

Carillon's advertising agency in the United States was bought out by a British group that handled other brands of spirits. Al Singer could no longer use the agency, so he went in search of a new one. More than one hundred agencies competed for the contract, but Michel Roux already favored the dynamic international agency that had been founded by his friend Bill Tragos and his partners in 1970. It was named TBWA after the initials of the four partners: Tragos, Claude Bonnange, Uli Wiesendanger, and Paolo Ajroldi, respectively a Greek-American, a Frenchman, a Swiss, and an Italian. Once it had passed the first selection stage, TBWA was able to attack the problem of the campaign's content. Two creative people from the New York agency, the South African Geoff Hayes and the Briton Graham Turner, were put to work. They began by using scenes from Swedish folklore, such as saunas and snowy landscapes, in a humorous way.

rent (it took many tries before the glass-makers were able to achieve the desired transparency), it would have no label (in contradiction of all the prevailing rules) but would be silkscreened with the necessary information, and a small engraved medallion would reproduce the image of L.O. Smith as a guarantee of authenticity.

Since the English word "absolute" could not be trademarked, the shorter Swedish version "absolut" was used, giving the vodka a more Swedish air.

Everything was ready for the launch, and the first shipment of Absolut Vodka left for the United States on April 17, 1979. The next step was to devise an advertising campaign that

But, once again, it was the "power of purity" message that would inspire the two men. One evening in November 1980, Hayes doodled a sketch of the bottle with a halo around it, with the caption "Absolut. The perfect vodka." The next day, Turner took up the idea, but went further with it, proposing the slogan "Absolut perfection." That was it. The two men made a series of sketches to show that this intangible formula—the bottle and just one word to accompany the name Absolut—had infinite possibilities. Today, more than five hundred versions of the concept have been produced by the agency and by many creative people with a variety of backgrounds.

To make the bottle irresistible, a then-unknown photographer, Steve Bronstein, had the idea of placing a piece of matt Plexiglas behind it with a lamp creating the effect of a nearly perfect halo. The campaign was launched at the end of 1980 and continues today with the same basic principles, setting a record for longevity in the advertising world. At the beginning, the ad was in black and white, with only the logo in blue. But humor and distance later came into play. On "Absolut Clarity," for example, a magnifying glass blew up the phrase "Country of Sweden" that is printed between "Absolut" and "Vodka." At the time, the USSR was in bad graces in the United States because of the war in Afghanistan and the destruction of a Korean airplane, and the ad stressed the fact that this was a vodka that was not at all Russian.

The simplicity, intelligence, and humor of the TBWA campaigns were quickly noticed on the American market, attracting yuppies and artistic and intellectual types. Within four years, sales grew from 10,000 to 440,000 cases.

CITIES, ART, FASHION, DESIGN

In 1984, the style of the Absolut campaigns passed another benchmark with "Absolut Stardom." For the first time, it was no longer the bottle itself that was photographed, but its silhouette, outlined by five thousand tiny blue and white lightbulbs. By then, the Absolut image was well enough known that it could be simply suggested. This qualitative leap allowed the use of anything and everything that could be transformed into the shape of the cult-bottle. A ski run in the mountains, the nineteenth round on a golf course, a printed circuit–anything was possible.

A fifteen-hectare field in Kansas, planted with different grains to represent the shape of the bottle, was even put to use. The photo was taken from a plane when the plants were suffi-

ciently ripe, and the resulting image was so graphic that some thought the whole thing had been done in a studio.

For "Absolut Harmony," 102 New York choristers were lined up on twenty-four levels in front of the Rockefeller Center Christmas tree, forming the shape of the famous bottle. This exploit was realized at sunset.

Then, in 1987, TBWA enriched its campaigns by creating the first series of ads. It all began with the need to increase the brand's renown in California. Tom McMannus, an art director, created an aerial photo of a swimming pool in the shape of the bottle and titled it "Absolut L.A." That is how Absolut won over Los Angeles. The ad was such a success that the same idea was applied to other American cities, including New York and Chicago, then to each state, and finally to the big cities in the rest of the world. For each of these impeccably produced ads, a key symbol of the place was transformed into the shape of the Absolut bottle. For Manhattan, it was Central Park, for New Orleans a trumpet, for Paris a Métro entrance, for Rome a scooter, and so on.

Another new direction had been taken in 1985 when the painter Andy Warhol became involved. He had already painted "La Grand Passion" for Grand Marnier liqueur, distributed in the United States by Michel Roux, who had become president of Carillon. Warhol offered to do another painting for Absolut, saying that although he did not drink alcohol, he loved the vodka, which he used as a perfume!

The amazing result was a painting of the Absolut bottle in black against a yellow background. Michel Roux wanted to use it for an ad in avant-garde magazines.

The success of the Warhol ad was such that it allowed him to hire other fashionable artists, including Keith Haring and Kenny Scharf. Then Absolut began using unknown artists, including painters, sculptors, and photographers.

All this began to interest collectors, who first accumulated the Absolut ads, then the derivative objects.

Next came the fashion designers, who dreamed up women's and men's clothing that carried the name Absolut or the silhouette of the bottle. The best designers thus contributed a new element to the trendy, chic world that

Absolut had created in less than ten years. Absolut also called on the great photographers (Newton, Lang, etc.) to take pictures of the creations of the great couturiers. Other designers began to make armchairs, couches, lamps, and stools in the shape of the Absolut bottle. Even *The New Yorker's* cartoonists made their contribution.

Sales reached 4.5 million cases in 1993, and 5.5 million in 1997. In the meantime, the distribution structure had changed in 1994, and Seagram had won the right to represent the chicken that had laid the golden egg on the international market. The first vodka to be imported onto the American market, Absolut was now present in Europe. Distribution had begun in Sweden only in 1981, two years after the American launch.

Proud of its purity, which it claims is more perfect than that of any other vodka, Absolut is still made exclusively in Ahus, a small, peaceful city with a population of 10,000. The vodka is rectified to the point where a small amount of less pure vodka must be added to give it a bit of flavor. But what really counts is the concept.

In addition to the vodka with a fifty percent alcohol content, flavored versions have been added to widen the market. The launch of Peppar, Lemon, and Kurrant led to a new frenzy of creative advertising campaigns dreamed up by the invincible TBWA agency.

Absolut Web sites have also flourished, many of them created by the vodka's fans, who keep each other informed about new Absolut campaigns and anything having to do with the vodka. A volume called *The Absolut Book* traces the history of the vodka.

One last example of the heights of luxury and modernity reached by Absolut: the operation conducted with the fashion designer Gianni Versace at the beginning of 1997. His exclusive designs, worn by top models, were photographed by Herb Ritts in an unusual setting: the Ice Hotel in Jukkäsjarvi, two hundred kilometers from the Arctic Circle in Sweden. This hotel is rebuilt every year with blocks of ice and snow. The campaign consists of eight astonishing photos, including one with Naomi Campbell embedded in a 2.4-meter-high bottle sculpted from a three-ton block of ice. It was a successful return to the source.

FINLAND

After having been the property of Sweden from the twelfth to eighteenth centuries, then of Russia until 1917, when it declared its independence, Finland was also dominated by its occupiers when it came to vodka.

It was supposedly the soldiers returning from a war in Russia who brought back to the country the first stills and the knowledge of how to make spirits from grain. For a long time, distilling was done at home clandestinely, and the practice spread quickly. By the eighteenth century, spirits are thought to have replaced beer as the most popular drink.

The first industrial distilleries were set up by Swedes, including Hans John Falkman, who worked for the Swedish royal court before moving to Helsinki in 1842 when the Swedish crown took over the monopoly rights to distillation.

In 1875, there were eighty-three distilleries in the country, and this growth was to continue. In 1880, a second yeast production unit–(necessary for the fermentation of the mash)–was set up at the Rajamäki distillery. Within ten years, it had become the country's major vodka company, called Puhdistettu Paloviina, meaning purified and burnt spirits.

Independence had hardly been won when in 1919 a period of general prohibition of alcohol began. The distilleries were nationalized and

closer to its Scandinavian neighbors and then to all of Western Europe. It became a member of the European Union in 1995. One of the conditions of membership (as for Sweden) was the ending of the state monopoly, which led to the appearance of new vodka producers.

THE LEADER: FINLANDIA

Relaunched in the 1950s, the Rajamäki distillery benefited from its use of pure water. Finlandia vodka was made there, created primarily for foreign markets, and especially the United States, in 1970. Finlandia opened up the American market to Scandinavian vodkas, which had been unknown on export markets, a full ten years before Absolut arrived to offer the idea of purity to American consumers.

Perhaps Finlandia did not have the advertising genius behind it that the Swedish vodka did, but its results were not negligible, with worldwide sales reaching 1.7 million cases in 1997, a fifty percent increase over 1993 sales.

Made exclusively of grains (malted and unmalted), Finlandia used a high-technology production process, multi-pressure distillation, that was invented in Finland and exported to other distillers, mainly in Scotland. After the cooking of the grain flour under pressure, the starch is transformed into sugar through the action of enzymes, then the whole is fermented by the action of selected yeasts. The mash, containing nine percent alcohol, is first distilled

Left: The marshes of the Lusmaniemi Inari Peninsula in northern Lapland, the land of ten thousand lakes. Below: Finlandia vodka was launched in Scandinavia in 1970 and on the American market in 1971. It is now sold in more than 80 countries.

the use of alcohol was suppressed, except for medicinal or industrial purposes.

As in the United States, illegal imports and the distillation of spirits known as "moonshine" became common.

In 1932, Prohibition ended, but the Finnish state retained its monopoly over the production of vodka and alcoholic liqueurs. A new distillery, Koskenkorva, was created in 1938.

The Rajamäki distillery, the oldest in the country, became famous for the production of the alcohol used to make Molotov cocktails, used by the partisans in their battles against Russian tanks and to run the motors of military vehicles.

After World War II, Finland was in a precarious position as a close neighbor of the Soviet Union. At first neutral, it gradually became

in a continuous still, then the resulting vapors (with thirty percent alcohol) pass through a condensation column and come out with a ninety-three percent alcohol content after the elimination of the fusel oils. It is then rectified in a continuous triple column to eliminate the methanol and the remaining impurities. The result contains ninety-six percent alcohol.

The alcohol is then carefully mixed with spring water from Rajamäki, which originates several dozen meters beneath the ground and owes its great purity to its origins in the nearby Arctic glaciers. Finlandia vodka is known for its great finesse, but also for its flavors of grains, appreciated by connoisseurs. Even the Russian Pokhlebkin, a fierce defender of his country's vodka, acknowledged the great quality of Finlandia, describing it as "exquisite, with a taste that is very different from that of Russian vodka."

Its original bottle evokes the Finnish glaciers and carries an image of white reindeer, the symbol of the country. A local saying holds that if you see the sun, the moon, and a white reindeer at the same time, all your wishes will be granted. A legend recounts the story of a young girl who was transformed into a white reindeer after a spell was cast on her. A group of hunters, her fiancé among them, began to chase her, and the fiancé was mortally wounded during the hunt. His blood broke the spell and the reindeer became once again the young woman. At that moment, the couple fell into profound, eternal sleep.

Since its creation, Finlandia has widened its range of products, with the appearance of original flavored vodkas: Cranberry and Pineapple. More recently, a luxury version was launched, called 21, to welcome in the new century. It comes in a superb bottle that looks like a perfume flacon.

Above and facing page: Located on an eighty-six-acre site, the ultramodern Koskenkorva distillery has some distilling columns that are ninety-six feet tall. The Primalco group makes use of every technological innovation and has an annual production capacity of more than one hundred million bottles.

The nationalized group Primalco, the successor to the former state monopoly, is still the major producer of Finnish vodka, with several other brands.

– Koskenkorva, the best-seller in Finland, was created in 1952 and has a distillery in the village of the same name, located in the heart of a vast grain-growing area. After distillation and rectification, the alcohol is transported to Rajamäki to be diluted with spring water. There are three versions of the vodka: forty percent alcohol, with a black label; fifty percent alcohol, with a silver label; and sixty percent alcohol, with a red label, sold mostly in duty-free outlets. Koskerkorvan Viina, with thirty-eight percent alcohol, is sweetened with three grams of sugar per liter.

– Viljavaakuna is a transparent vodka with forty percent alcohol and a smoother flavor.

– Leijonaviina, a transparent vodka, has thirty-two percent alcohol and is dry in taste.

– Pöytäviina is transparent and contains thirty-eight percent alcohol, with three grams of sugar added to each liter.

– Dry Vodka is grain-based and transparent, with forty percent alcohol.

– Maximus is transparent, with forty percent alcohol.

– Tähkäviina, with forty-two percent alcohol, has a yellowish color due to the addition of distilled malt.

– Riistaryyppy, a colorless schnapps with thirty-eight percent alcohol, is fairly sweet, with ten grams of sugar added per liter.

THE NEW PRODUCERS

Since the end of the state monopoly in 1995, new brands made by independent distillers have appeared on the Finnish market.

– Lignell & Piispanen, founded by two pharmacists in the city of Kuopio in 1882, became famous for its liqueur made with Arctic raspberries. In spite of Prohibition and the state monopoly, the company was able to survive by producing aromatic extracts for the food industry. In 1995, it brought back Savon Wiina (an alcohol from Savon, a province of Finland), which had been very popular before Prohibition. This colorless vodka contains thirty-eight percent alcohol. It is fairly dry and made exclu-

Finland has an area of around 130,000 square miles, including 77,220 square miles of forests. Its national symbol is the reindeer.

sively of grain. The company also launched Marskin Ryyppy, a colorless, delicately flavored liqueur named after Marshall Mannerheim, the hero of Finland's struggle against the Russians.

– Chymos, a producer of fruit juices and other food products (such as jams), has turned to the distillation of spirits, notably Pohjan Poika Vodka, whose name refers to the Finnish trappers who used to crisscross Finland's lakes and forests in search of fur. This colorless vodka, with thirty-eight percent alcohol, has no added sugar. A second version contains fifty-nine percent alcohol.

– Cheveleff, founded in 1992, has a presence in many countries and deals in a variety of products, including cigarettes, clothing, and jewelry. It also sells Cheveleff vodka (distilled by Lignell & Piispanen), whose modern-style bottle has a sailing theme.

– Marli, based in Turku, sells the grain-based Nordfors Viina, with a thirty-eight percent alcohol content.

– Sahti-Mafia makes Pontikka ("moonshine"), a strong, transparent vodka with a fifty percent alcohol content. Its name is a reference to the clandestine distillation that used to be done at night. It also produces a traditional Finnish beer, Sahti.

DENMARK

Like the other Northern European countries, Denmark learned to distill spirits in the fifteenth century, or perhaps even earlier–(a rudimentary still dating to the fourteenth century has been found).

While some grains were used, potatoes were the most common raw material, and for a long time, distillation was mostly a family activity. In the middle of the nineteenth century, there were around two thousand distilleries in the country. Industrialization and the institution of a monopoly later led to a marked decrease in their number.

Denmark differed from its neighbors in its development of a particular style of flavored spirit, aquavit, which continues to be the preferred drink of Danish consumers (see the chapter on aquavit).

The production of transparent vodka remains marginal, even though new brands have recently appeared, mostly for export, since aquavit does not sell well on export markets.

The Danisco Distillers group is today the largest Danish producer and the only one that makes rectified alcohol, in its distilleries in Aalborg, Grena, and Jutland, which it also resells to other private liquor makers. The group has grown through the gradual absorption of independent distillers, beginning in 1881 with the Aalborg distillery, where the first quality aquavits were made in 1846 by Isidor Hennius.

Today, the group is part of a huge conglomerate of farm-produce industries, Danisco A/S.

Among the wide range of spirits produced by the group, there are two brands of transparent vodkas:

- Frïs Vodka was developed in the middle of the 1980s, with the goal of offering a flavorful vodka that would have a rich texture as soon as it came out of the freezer. The Danish word *frïs* means "ice" or "frost." Its production is fairly complicated, and the goal is to obtain a pure spirit that also has real flavor. The distillation technique, which has been patented, includes several rectification steps, as well as the chilling of the alcoholic vapors to minimize the amount of impurities, which freeze before the alcohol. The process also involves several filtrations, notably through charcoal, which give it its characteristically smooth texture. After dilution with water of great purity, the vodka contains forty percent alcohol. It is sold by a joint venture between Danisco Distillers and the American group Hiram Walker, which has been providing access to the North American market since 1992. It is also distributed in Japan through

agreements with the Suntory group.

- Danzka Vodka is a more classic pure-grain spirit that follows international standards. It was purchased in 1994 by Danisco Distillers. Well-known in Denmark, it is also well-distributed on Latin American markets and in the duty-free network. Made in Aalborg with demineralized water and containing forty percent alcohol, Danzka is filtered several times, notably through charcoal, before it is bottled. It is sold in three versions: neutral and flavored with lemon or blackcurrant.

The eighteen Fareoe ("Foroyar" in the local language) Islands, also known as the "Sheep Islands," form an archipelago and have been self-governing dependencies of Denmark since 1948.

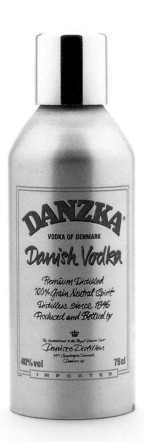

NORWAY

The kingdom of the Vikings, who crisscrossed the seas of Northern Europe and even reached America well before Christopher Columbus, had to wait a long time before achieving independence. It became a province of Denmark in 1380, then became dependent on Sweden in 1814, while retaining a good deal of autonomy. The country did not become fully independent until 1905.

The first reference to spirits in Norway is found in a letter addressed to the archbishop of Bergen, Olav Engel-

and wines, leading to the disappearance of the last independent producers.

This company existed until 1996. Unlike its Scandinavian neighbors, Norway is not a member of the European Union, but the need to liberalize its economy led to the opening up of the market. Two public companies took over the activities of the former monopoly, with Arcus Produkter for production and Arcus Distribusjon for distribution.

Aquavit accounts for the largest part

brekston, dated 1531. The country developed its own particular style of strong alcohol with powerful flavors. The Danes contributed aquavit (*akevit* in Norwegian), which continues to dominate today. Potatoes were always used, along with grains, and distillation was common. In 1840, a census counted at least 9,000 stills in this sparsely populated country.

But the pressure of the Lutheran Church and technological improvements soon put an end to domestic production, and ten years later the number of home stills was reduced to five hundred.

In 1922, independent Norway created a state monopoly, A/S Vinmonopolet, to produce and distribute spirits

of Norwegian spirits, but several brands of transparent, unflavored vodkas have been developed by Arcus Produkter.

Hammer took the name of a former Norwegian distiller, Christopher Blix Hammer (1720-1804). This is a transparent, grain-based vodka with an alcohol content of 42.7 percent. Two flavored versions are produced, one with lemon and one with pepper, and the company also makes gin.

Vikingfjord Vodka, one of the latest creations of Arcus Produkter, was conceived especially for the export market. After rectification, this very pure vodka is mixed with pure water from Arctic glaciers, which explains why it is called "glacial vodka."

Facing page:
A Spitzberg landscape.
Above: A fishing port on
the Hardanger Fjord in
southern Norway.
Left: The Lofoten
Islands, located north
of the Arctic Circle.
Below: a typical scene
in the northern county
of Finnmark.

THE BALTIC COUNTRIES

The three Baltic countries, Estonia, Latvia, and Lithuania, were long dominated by foreign powers, from the Teutonic Knights to Sweden, Germany, and the Soviet Union, preventing them from developing specific types of spirits or vodka. A state distillery founded in 1900 in Latvia made a range of vodkas, mostly from potatoes, but it was nationalized by the Soviets after the annexation of the Baltic countries in 1940.

Since independence in 1991, after the fall of Soviet communism, the manufacture of spirits has started up again in the Baltic countries.

In Estonia, Liviko Distilleries in Tallinn produces several types of vodka. Eesti Viin, with thirty-eight percent alcohol, is smooth, sweet, and highly aromatic. Viru Valge, made of grain and enriched with sugar during bottling, has forty percent alcohol. Monopole is made by the Remedia group and contains 37.5 percent alcohol.

In Latvia, most production is controlled by a once-nationalized company, which has been partially privatized since. It makes several types of high-quality schnapps, the preferred alcoholic drink of the Latvians, as well as several brands of grain-based vodkas: Kristal Dzidrais, Rigas Originalais, Zelta, Favorits, Rigalya, and Monopols. The latter two claim to rival the best international vodkas in terms of purity and quality.

Left: The city of Vilnius in Lithuania.
Below left: Tallinn, Estonia.

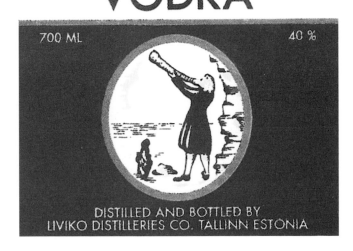

123

AQUAVIT

Basically, aquavit and schnapps are the same as vodka. They are made of the same raw materials (grains and/or potatoes) and with the same distillation techniques, and are seldom aged. For aquavit especially, flavoring is more common, but this characteristic is also found in some Polish vodkas. In fact, the only reason that the aquavits of Denmark and Scandinavia and the schnapps of Germany have their own denomination is that they have a strong national character. They are considered an important element of local culture and were chosen above others as signs of belonging to a common heritage. The fact that they so closely resemble the vodkas of neighboring counties makes no difference.

Aquavit, a Scandinavian cousin of vodka, hardly differs from its relative. Both use the same raw materials (especially potatoes) and distillation techniques.

ISIDOR HENNIUS'S INVENTION

Aquavit (also spelled "akvavit") is the Danish transcription of *aqua vitae,* or "water of life" in Latin. Unlike other spirits, we know exactly who invented it: Isidor Hennius, a young distiller who moved to the city of Aalborg on the Jutland peninsula in Denmark in 1848.

Until then, the history of the distillation of spirits in Denmark had been very similar to that of neighboring Northern European countries. The technique became known at the end of the fifteenth century and spread rapidly, with both families and farms setting up home stills. The lack of grains in the country forced distillers to also make use of potatoes. A local proverb holds that with one potato, one can always make a small glass of spirits. In the first half of the nineteenth century, the Danish state decided to increase its control over the production of spirits and set up a monopoly. Nevertheless, more than two thousand distillers were counted in the country at the time.

Isidor Hennius, the inventor of aquavit, was the first in Denmark to use a continuous still and to rectify the alcohol.

When Isidor Hennius arrived in Aalborg, the city was the main distilling center because it was located in the middle of a grain-growing region. His personal recipe, which was to become a great success, is not precisely known. We know only that part of its particular flavor comes from a strong aromatization with cumin. Hennius was the first distiller in Denmark to use a continuous still and to practice rectification to obtain the greatest possible purity and to eliminate undesirable elements

The popularity of this aquavit was so great that it quickly adopted the name of its native city, Aalborg, which it still carries today. It is made by the Danisco Distillers group, the largest producer of spirits (with several vodkas and various liqueurs) in Denmark.

The making of traditional aquavit is a little more complex than that of other grain-based spirits. A neutral *eau-de-vie* (made of grain or potatoes) is used to macerate various aromatic plants and spices, especially cumin. The result is distilled to obtain an aromatic extract that is then mixed with water and neutral spirits. This mixture then rests for several weeks before being bottled.

Aalborg, the most popular brand, is a fairly strong *eau-de-vie*, with forty-five percent alcohol, but it is very mellow and has a great richness. Cumin dominates its flavoring.

In 1946, for the centenary of the distillery, an aquavit called Jubilaeums was created. With a yellow-gold color and forty-two percent alcohol, its flavoring is more complex, dominated by cumin, dill, and coriander.

Other brands sold on the Danish market include:

- Brondum Kummen, created at the end of the nineteenth century by the distiller Anton Brondum in Copenhagen. Its cumin and cinnamon flavoring have made it a great success.

- Harald Jensen, with forty-five percent alcohol, is another highly aromatic aquavit, launched in 1883.

- Holger Denske, a more recent aquavit, is made by the distiller Oskar Davidsen in Copenhagen for Taster Wine A/S, a wine-importing group founded in 1946 by Fritz Paustian. The standard version contains thirty-eight percent alcohol, and the pale yellow Guld contains forty percent. Both are pleasantly flavored with cumin.

While aquavit can be drunk straight, it is most commonly consumed with a traditional Danish smörgasbord– various smoked fishes, charcuterie, and cheeses served as canapés.

Norway also developed its own style of aquavit, marked above all by the country's maritime tradition. The distillation of potato- or grain-based *eaux-de-vie*, flavored with cumin, goes back at least two centuries, as is proved by a treatise published in 1776 by Christopher Hammer, a landowner who conducted chemistry experiments. In particular, he studied the effects of different aromatic herbs, especially cumin, either used alone or mixed with others.

The major contribution of the Norwegians to the making of aquavit dates to the nineteenth century and was the result of an unexpected discovery. A Norwegian boat, the brig "Trondheim Prove," set out in 1805 on a long journey to India and Australia, carrying aquavit in a few small barrels that had once held sherry. The aquavit was to be sold at the ship's destinations, along with other merchandise, but it was not a great commercial success, and the ship returned to Norway with most of its cargo of aquavit intact. On arrival, it was discovered that this unplanned aging, accelerated by the movements of the ship, had created an *eau-de-vie* of a lovely golden color that was especially mellow and aromatic. The ship belonged to the Lysholm family, and the secret of this high-quality *eau-de-vie* was carefully guarded until 1821, when Jorgen B. Lysholm

founded a distillery in the city of Trondheim. Using the traditional recipes for the making of aquavit, he institutionalized the family recipe, sending his barrels off on ships going to India and Australia. He called the aquavit aged in this way Linie, a reference to the "crossing of the line," the Equator.

The family business was later nationalized, and it has now become the private group Arcus, a large producer of spirits. Linie no longer travels around the world in sailboats. Since 1927, the Norwegian company Wilhelmsen has been responsible for the procedure, specifying that the barrels must travel under the bridge of the ship and that the voyage should last at least four-and-a-half months. Each bottle of aquavit thus made carries the name of the ship on which it traveled on a band around its neck.

Lysholm Linie is the best-known brand of the Arcus group, which produces other varieties of aquavit with different flavorings.

Arcus's Loiten Export, an aquavit made according to another procedure (a mixture of neutral aquavit with aromatic plants), also travels the world in oak barrels before being bottled.

THE REST OF THE WORLD

The development of vodka outside of Northern Europe, where it originated, is relatively recent, coming far later than that of other spirits like cognac and whiskey. It was only after World War II that vodka began to be consumed around the world, especially in the United States.

Smirnoff, launched by Heublein, was largely responsible for this development, paving the way for many imitations in the Western world. Because of the communist regime in most of the vodka-making countries (especially Russia and Poland), the name "vodka" was never legally protected as a designation of the origin or quality of what was in the bottle. This means that what are essentially colorless alcohols, usually with a neutral taste, can be made and sold anywhere in the world under the name vodka. These spirits bear little resemblance to what is still made today in Poland, Russia, and the Scandinavian countries.

Some may find this situation deplorable, but it is difficult to imagine a return to the past, in spite of the efforts of some countries, including Russia, to re-establish the primacy of their rights over the definition of vodka and its origins.

With a few exceptions, these international vodkas are usually not bad products. True, they often lack personality, but they are mostly satisfactory as a cocktail ingredient, which is how they are used by consumers.

Left: A bartender at the Red Square bar in Miami. Above: Richard Branson shows off Virgin vodka.

The development of vodka around the world owes a great deal to the Bolshevik Revolution of 1917, although this was surely not one of the concerns of Lenin and his followers when they took power in Saint Petersburg and Moscow.

The victory of the revolutionaries led to the exodus of many Russians, especially the aristocrats, many of whom had little to take with them except their names and, in a few cases, some knowledge of distilling. Under the czars, the monopoly on the making of spirits was often entrusted to the nobles. The case of Vladimir Smirnov is the most obvious example, but he was not the only one; the Gorbatschow family, who left Russia for Berlin in 1921, and Alexander Eristoff can also be cited.

This development was not easy, since neither Europeans nor Americans took much interest in vodka at the time. They were not exactly lacking for alcoholic beverages, for they had had their own for a long time, with their characteristic flavors and well-established drinking customs.

Top: Smirnoff, the world's top-selling vodka, has become the second-best-selling brand of spirits, after Bacardi rum.

To make themselves known and appreciated, other vodka-makers followed the route mapped out by Smirnoff, creating vodkas with a more or less neutral flavor and allusions to Russia on the label, such as family coats of arms or designs dating to the time of the czars. These vodkas found their place in the still relatively open market for cocktails.

Cocktails, or mixed drinks that combine one or more alcoholic beverages with various fruit or vegetable juices, are a fairly recent invention. The oldest date from the nineteenth century, but they were consumed mostly by a wealthy elite. Their popularization began with American Prohibition, when the Americans, deprived of alcohol, discovered the paradise of the West Indies, especially Cuba, where many recipes mixed rum with tropical fruit juices and cane sugar.

After World War II, the Western world was hungry for novelties and went looking for new taste sensations. The traditional alcoholic beverages like whiskey and cognac have strong flavors and a dark color that limit their use in the making of cocktails because they overwhelm the taste of the other ingredients. With vodka or gin, which have less powerful flavors, sometimes to the point of neutrality, it is the flavors of the fruits, liqueurs, syrups, or spices that dominate. In a cocktail, spirits are of interest primarily for their alcoholic content.

With the success of Smirnoff, which within a few years became one of the best-selling alcohol brands in the world, other distillers quickly understood the importance of the new market that was opening up to them. A further encouragement was the fact that vodka is particularly easy to fabricate: any grain can be used to make it, even the least expensive ones such as corn. Its continuous distillation is followed by

When Gorbachev was the first secretary of the Communist Party, he initiated several measures to tax vodka sales. That hasn't stopped him, however, from helping to sell Karkov vodka in the streets of Minneapolis.

rectification, and it requires pure water to dilute the distilled alcohol to the appropriate strength (37.5 percent to 40 percent alcohol in volume). There is no need to age it, and there are no storage costs. Once it is bottled, the product is ready to be sold.

The most important step with vodka is marketing. At first, a Russian connection was considered essential–a Russian-sounding name, for example, preferably ending in "off," "ov," or "ski." Another trick was to use a well-known name that was not trademarked, such as Tolstoy, Prince Igor, or Popov (a great success in the United States). Another approach, often used by the British, is to add a vodka to an existing line of liquors with a name that is already well-known to consumers, as was done by Gilbey's, Gordon's, and Burnett's. This ensures space on store shelves for the vodka, leaving little room for more authentic vodkas that might be interesting to real vodka lovers but whose names mean nothing to most consumers.

NORTH AMERICA

The names of the several dozen vodkas made on the North American continent, in both the United States and Canada, range from A to Z (Alexi to Zhenka). They include the famous Smirnoff and Popov as well as relatively unknown brands made by small regional producers, who often add a vodka to their range of liquors.

Most of them are very similar to each other and, like Smirnoff, are essentially colorless alcohols with fairly neutral flavors.

The important thing for these markets is not the intrinsic qualities of the vodkas, but the image that they project. At the time of the Cold War, drinking Smirnoff, with its label that evoked the czars, was a symbolic way of braving

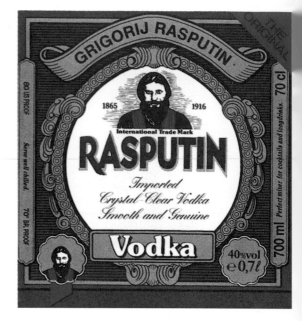

the Soviet menace. A little later, Absolut sales skyrocketed about the time that a Korean airline was shot down by the Soviets–the reasoning being that Absolut had nothing to do with Russia. The fact that Sweden is practically unknown to most Americans was not a problem, and in any case the advertising campaign created by the TBWA agency never attempted to make any connection between Absolut and Scandinavia, apart from a few oblique references.

Another theme that is increasingly used by American producers is that of purity, perhaps because of the success of Absolut. Among the brands that play up that essential ingredient, water, are Crater Lake, Devil's Springs, Everclear, Frost, Glacier Bay, Mad River, Rain, Silver Creek, and Teton River.

Lately, however, there has been a new interest in traditional vodkas, as is shown by the success of the Russian vodka Stolichnaya. Like Absolut, which has many fans on the Internet, there are many lively Web sites dedicated to "Stoli." But, once again, the effect of fashion, with all its excesses, is mainly based on interest in the vodka itself. Above all, vodka is an important ingredient for the making of cocktails of all types, and, in North America, only the purest vodkas are consumed. Their characteristic flavors are not important; what matters is that they have a high alcohol content and can be mixed with orange juice, tomato juice, or vermouth.

There are, however, a few American vodkas

that are out of the ordinary, if not for their flavor, then for their history.

– Inferno. This fairly new Canadian brand is unusual in that it is packaged in a 75-centiliter glass jug containing two red chili peppers, which give it its fiery character. It belongs to the "911" variety, and according to the Scoville scale (which measures the level of capsaicin, the irritant that provides the sensation of hotness), it has an average strength of between 2,500 and 5,000, while stronger varieties run between 100,000 and 300,000 units. The peppers are macerated for at least three weeks in a vodka that has been distilled four times and filtered through charcoal. Bloody Marys made with this vodka do not need any added Tabasco sauce. The chili peppers can be eaten once the vodka has been finished.

The Kittling Ridge group, based in Ontario, not far from Niagara Falls, produces and/or sells a wide range of wines and spirits, including another brand of vodka, Prince Igor.

– Skyy. This vodka was invented by Maurice Kanbar in October 1993 to prevent headaches in drinkers. An industrialist and inventor, he was tired of getting headaches after having drunk a few vodka-based cocktails or one or two glasses of wine, so he set out to create the purest vodka possible by perfecting a four-column still that eliminates all undesirable elements, which he calls "congenerics," claiming that they are responsible for headaches and hangovers. This health claim has not been well-received by everyone, especially the Bureau of Alcohol, Tobacco and Firearms, but it helps to explain the rapid success of the new vodka, which may also be due to the elaborate design of the handsome cobalt-blue bottle. The same color was used in the advertising campaigns that followed its launch. Distilled in the Midwest, Skyy Vodka is

made of grains, bottled in San Francisco (where the company is headquartered), and contains forty percent alcohol. It has a clean and fairly mellow taste.

– Smirnoff Silver. In addition to the different varieties of Smirnoff made in various distilleries around the world, this one comes directly from Connecticut, Smirnoff's first American outpost. It contains 45.2 percent alcohol.

– Wolfschmidt. This was the name of a family of distillers who had been based in Riga, Latvia since 1847. Their vodkas were a great success: they were the official suppliers of czars Alexander II and Nicholas II, and they were probably the first to export vodka to the United States at the beginning of the twentieth century. The company now belongs to the bourbon maker Jim Beam. This pure-grain vodka has a forty percent alcohol content and sells more than a million cases on the American market.

EUROPE

In addition to Russia, Central Europe, and Scandinavia, vodka is made in other European countries. Most often, this came about when existing distillers added to their range of beverages an *eau-de-vie*, usually colorless and neutral tasting, in order to respond to market demand. Others were more original in their approach.

Austria. The country's proximity to Central Europe explains the existence of a few local brands, such as the rather bitter 1777 Lviv, inspired by a Ukrainian recipe, and Monopolowa.

Belorussia. Poland and Russia long fought over the possession of this former Soviet republic, which has its own vodka producers, notably the brands Ababycabl (made in the capital, Minsk), Leader, Legend, and Old Warrior.

France. Eristoff, with its far-off Russian origins, has no real national identity. It belonged for many years to the Italian group Martini and is now part of Bacardi, one of the world leaders. This neutral vodka has a 37.5 percent alcohol content, and more than eight million bottles are made and distributed each year in several countries, including France. It is found in many European countries, as well as in North America, in its original bottle with a slightly flared base. The name comes from an old noble Ukrainian family, once known as Eristhavi, but was changed to the more Russian-sounding Eristoff in the middle of the century. Constantine Eristhavi created the recipe for the vodka in 1806 in Novgorod, then passed it on to his son Alexander and eventually to his grandson

Nicholas, who then sold it to the Benedictine company, which was later taken over by Martini.

Grey Goose Vodka is made by the cognac maker Mounier and is exclusively distributed on the American market by Sidney Frank of New Rochelle. Made of wheat, rye, and barley, it is distilled in four stages, contains forty percent alcohol, and comes in a pretty bottle with a satiny surface. It was the only vodka served on board the Concorde during a special flight between New York and Bordeaux for the 1997 Vinexpo trade fair.

"La Vodka" is a brand distilled in France by a Bordeaux-region producer.

Germany. Gorbatschow, the most common brand, has nothing to do with the last secretary-general of the Soviet Communist Party. It is named after a family of distillers from Saint Petersburg who fled the Bolshevik regime in 1921 and went into business in Berlin, where they intended to supply vodka to other Russian refugees. The brand now belongs to Henkell, a large producer of effervescent wines. It comes in different strengths, with 37.5, 40, 50, and 60 percent alcohol.

The Dethleffsen group, a major producer of spirits that has been around for more than 250 years, makes the Rasputin brand of vodka. Decorated with the image of the famous monk who haunted the court of the last czar, this vodka exists in transparent versions (with 37.5, 40 and 70 percent alcohol) and in versions flavored with lemon and cranberry.

Other vodkas have

names that allude to the Russian world–such as Puschkin of the IB Berentzen group, which comes in both neutral and flavored versions–and to Germany, such as Bismarck. There is even one named after Karl Marx.

Great Britain. In addition to the brands made by gin producers (Gilbey's, Gordon's, Tanqueray, etc.), which often carry the company name, there are several other British vodkas:

– Black Death. The macabre name and the skull wearing a top hat on the label might lead you to believe that this is an extra-strong vodka, but it contains only forty percent alcohol.

– Selekt. A fairly neutral grain vodka, destined primarily for the Russian and duty-free markets.

– Vladivar. Originally made by a small brewery and then sold to the Whyte & Mackay group, this vodka was launched with an ironic advertising campaign featuring, for example, a parade of Soviet troops on Red Square in Moscow.

– Virgin. In addition to Richard Branson's activities in fields as diverse as the record business, aviation and cola, his group also has a range of vodkas with alcohol contents of 37.5, 40, and 50 percent, made by the whiskey distiller William Grant.

Ireland. Irish Distillers, the largest producer of spirits in the Republic of Ireland, makes a vodka called Hussar.

Italy. The country produces mostly light vodkas with between twenty-five percent and thirty percent

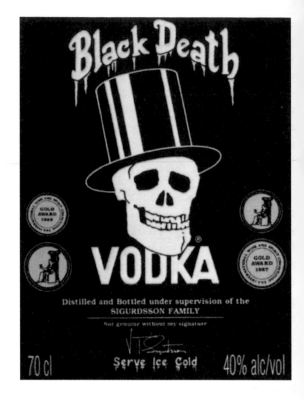

alcohol, usually flavored with fruits or plants. The Zucco group, which makes several liqueurs, including the famous Amaretto Disaronno, has been making the Artic range of vodkas since 1997. All but the pure vodka, with forty percent alcohol, contain twenty-five percent alcohol. There are no less than eleven ver-

sions flavored with fruit juices, ranging from pineapple to peach, banana, lemon, melon, and mint, which come in a bottle created by the designer Bertone.

They are similar to the Keglevich vodkas, made by Stock, which contain thirty percent alcohol and are flavored with lemon, peach, and melon, and to the peach-flavored Liudka, with twenty-seven percent alcohol.

The Netherlands. The Dutch invented industrial distillation, and, not surprisingly, they call some of their spirits "vodka," including Ketel One, a grain vodka made by the Nolet distillery. Founded in Schiedam in 1691, the distillery has been owned by the same family for ten generations. This original vodka is made in the traditional way in a pot still, which lends it a remarkable mellowness. It is now widely exported, especially to the United States.

Ursus (which means "bear" in Latin), is a brand made according to a recipe created in Ireland when distillation was illegal there. It belongs today to the De Hoorn group and also comes in lemon- and blackcurrant-flavored versions.

Royalty became the official supplier to Queen Beatrix in 1988 and carries the Dutch royal arms. Made by the Hooghoudt de Groningue distillery in the north of the country, it comes in a blue bottle, a sign of its "nobility and dignity." It is filtered through coal made from peat.

Scotland. Like London's gin producers, Scottish whiskey makers have not been able to resist the temptation to make vodka. Among them are Grant's, with a vodka of the same name; and the Campbell group, with the Karinskaya brand, which contains 37.5 percent alcohol and was formerly distributed by the Pernod-Ricard group.

Ukraine. In spite of its long attachment to the former USSR, Ukraine has always held on to its own style of vodka, called *gorilka* (which means "burning»), the favorite drink of the Cossacks of Dniepr. Instead of being made from rye, as Moscow vodkas are, it is made with wheat and flavored with lime-blossom honey. There are several different brands, along with many Moscow-style vodkas.

ENJOYING VODKA

The two main families of vodka, the traditional and the modern, are consumed in two different ways: straight, sometimes with a meal, or mixed in a wide variety of cocktails. The first method is practiced primarily in Central and Northern Europe, where vodka originated, while the second is more common in North America and the rest of the world.

Left: Whether beluga, sevruga or osetra, caviar is the perfect accompaniment to vodka. Above: While they don't bring out the specific flavors of vodka, cocktails have helped popularize it around the world.

TRADITIONAL USES

In Central and Northern Europe, vodka is traditionally drunk straight, usually served very cold or even iced. Ideally, the bottle should be kept in the freezer, as is done in Russian restaurants, where it is brought to the table enveloped in a block of ice. Glasses can be kept in the refrigerator to keep the vodka cold longer.

Vodka is the only type of alcohol that is commonly refrigerated. When it is cold, the taste of the alcohol is diminished in the mouth, and the dominant aroma is brought out, especially when the vodka is made of rye.

This practice is not advised for all vodkas, however, especially flavored ones from Poland or Russia. These are served at room

Vodka is best appreciated ice-cold and served in small glasses.

temperature so their aromatic qualities can be appreciated. Some, like Polish krupnik, are even served warm to bring out the flavors of the spices and honey they contain.

The traditional image, which has become something of a cliché, shows the consumer drinking his shot of vodka in one gulp and even, in the case of the Russians, tossing the empty glass over his shoulder before taking another. This practice is most commonly used on ceremonial occasions, punctuated by the toast "to your health."

Vodka is often sipped, however, so that its special qualities can be better appreciated. Small, narrow glasses that contain no more than five centiliters are used in both these cases.

In another traditional practice, the drinker bites into a slice of lemon covered with powdered sugar after downing the vodka. In the mouth, and especially on the gums, the sweet-sour combination contrasts with the strength of the alcohol and increases its effects.

This convivial drinking method is usually practiced before a meal. Vodka can also be served as an after-dinner drink, especially the highly flavored ones.

VODKA AND FOOD

Vodka goes extremely well with traditional Russian, Polish, and Scandinavian dishes, not just because the products come from the same region, but also because they harmonize so well. Vodka quickly quenches the thirst after the consumption of the salty, peppery, and highly flavored traditional cuisines of these countries. The fiery taste of vodka also provides a good counterbalance to the fat of smoked fish or charcuterie. Vodka also aids in the digestion of these often copious and sometimes heavy dishes.

Some foods are even made of the same ingredients that go into vodka; rye bread goes well with Zytnia vodka, for example, or *blinis* with wheat-based vodka.

Russian *zakuski* (*zakaski* in Polish) are made of a variety of traditional dishes that are good accompaniments to vodka. These cold and hot snacks are served before a meal. Their original purpose was to keep guests occupied while the main meal was being prepared in the kitchen, and they were laid out on a special table from which the guests served themselves.

Zakuski are made up primarily of caviar and smoked fish eggs, served on bite-sized pieces of buttered black bread; scooped-out loaves of rye bread filled with sauerkraut and slices of smoked goose; piroski, small pastries with various fillings; marinated or smoked fish (salmon, eel, and sturgeon); meatballs; herring pâté; deviled eggs; salads made with fish, poultry, beets, potatoes, and fine herbs; sweet

In Moscow, a vodka tasting accompanied by pickles.

and sour pickles; and beets, plums, and mushrooms marinated in vinegar. A choice of breads, mostly rye, sometimes flavored with cumin, onion, or poppyseeds, is served as well.

It might seem shocking to those who are weary of alcoholism that vodka is also drunk along with the main meal in Central or Northern Europe. Obviously, moderation is possible, but it must also be kept in mind that a small glass of vodka (five centiliters) is equal to a normal glass of wine (eighteen centiliters). In addition, the great diversity of the flavors of vodka, from the driest to the sweetest, with added nuances of pepper, lemon, and spices, offers a vast choice of gastronomic combinations.

TWO TRADITIONAL POLISH VODKA RECIPES

These two recipes for homemade flavored vodkas are from the book Savoureuse Pologne *(Editions Noir sur Blanc) by Viviane Bourdon. They serve as a reminder that in Poland, vodka is a integral element of everyday life.*

HONEY VODKA (KRUPNIK)

Krupnik can be drunk hot and is especially appropriate in winter for its warming qualities. Since it is difficult to filter, it is preferable to macerate the spices separately. It is normally prepared with an alcohol of ninety degrees, then diluted to half that with water, but a forty-five degree alcohol can also be used.

INGREDIENTS: 1 LITER (1 QUART) OF 45° ALCOHOL, 200 GRAMS (7 OUNCES) OF HONEY, 1 CINNAMON STICK, 5 SMALL JAMAICAN RED PEPPERS, 1/2 TSP POWDERED GINGER, 1 MACE, 1 VANILLA POD.

Cover spices with alcohol and store in an airtight jar. Let steep for two weeks. Shake frequently. When ready, melt the honey over low heat in a large sauce pan. Gradually raise the heat until the honey foams. Maintain the temperature, skimming if necessary, until the honey clarifies. Remove from heat. Pour the alcohol into the hot honey. Mix well while adding the spice mixture. Store in airtight bottles in a cool place. After at least six months of aging, the krupnik will be flavorful and clear. Strain before serving.

CHERRY VODKA (WISNIOWKA)

Cherry vodka strongly resembles a liqueur and can be served after dinner, although this practice is becoming rare in Poland. The macerated fresh fruits dilute the alcohol, so it is important to use a ninety degree alcohol. Anything weaker will result in a creamy liquor that is lacking in punch.

INGREDIENTS: 1 KILOGRAM (2.2 POUNDS) BLACK CHERRIES, 1 LITER (1 QUART) 90° ALCOHOL, 600 GRAMS (3 CUPS) SUGAR, 7 GRAMS (1/4 OUNCE) MACE.

Wash the cherries, but do not pit them. Add the mace, cover with alcohol and seal in an airtight glass container. Let steep for one week, stirring daily. Strain the liquid into another jar, cover, and store in a cool place.

Add the sugar to the cherries in their original container. Seal and place in the sun or in a warm place. Stir every two or three days. After a few weeks, the fruit will have digested the sugar. Strain and pour the syrup into the macerated alcohol. Wash the cherries in 15 centiliters (5 fluid ounces) of boiling water and add this liquid to the vodka to reduce its alcohol content.

Repeat the process. Let the resulting mixture rest for one month, then strain into serving bottles.

Caviar and other fish eggs are also perfect accompaniments to vodka; these two summits of Russian gastronomy suit each other to a tee. The best Muscovite vodkas enhance the creaminess of beluga caviar, with its hint of hazelnut flavor, or the sweetness of osetra caviar, with its less fishy flavor. The saltier sevruga is mellowed by a quality vodka.

Smoked or marinated salmon, a Scandinavian delicacy, is the perfect partner of a good Swedish or Polish vodka. Zubrowka is the first choice, but aquavit is another good option.

Herring, the king of the Baltic, goes perfectly with vodkas made on its banks. The culinary traditions of the different Baltic countries have found many ways to treat herring: salted, smoked, marinated in vinegar, fried, in a pâté, etc. Herring is traditionally accompa-

Vodka can also be used in the preparation of certain dishes. Salmon marinated in Zubrowka, for example, takes on new flavors. Another classic use of vodka, as with other spirits, is in flambéed dishes. Flavored vodkas (especially with pepper, blackcurrant, or lemon) add their specific aromas to sauces. Fried meat, for example, can be deglazed with a little pepper vodka. Or a small amount of lemon vodka can be added to baked fish. Even those who don't drink alcohol can enjoy these dishes because the alcohol evaporates entirely during cooking.

Flavored vodkas can also be used to make desserts, especially ice cream or sorbets, or to bring out the flavor of a fruit sauce, especially ones made with red fruits, using a blackcurrant vodka, for example.

While caviar is the perfect mate to vodka, smoked or marinated salmon and cabbage are also good companions.

nied by potatoes (in a salad in Poland), which of course is the raw material of many vodkas.

Sweet or sour cream is often served with these fish and offers an especially interesting counterpoint to vodka, softening its bite while bringing out its flavors.

The use of the same raw materials (rye, wheat, or barley) in vodka and bread (or, in Russia, the *blini*) can make for interesting combinations.

Finally, cabbage, one of the basic foodstuffs of Central Europe, goes very well with vodka, whether it is served raw, in a salad, or marinated as sauerkraut. Its strong flavors correspond to the strength of the vodka.

VODKA COCKTAILS

The simplest addition to vodka is a few ice cubes, which chill and dilute it as they melt.

While vodka is rarely mixed with other ingredients in its countries of origin, the cocktail was the primary vector for its consumption in the rest of the world. Orange juice (it is said that its use became popular during American Prohibition as a way of disguising the bad taste of bootlegged alcohol), tomato juice, and many other beverages–some alcoholic, some not–gradually became associated with vodka thanks to imaginative bartenders.

These flavored, aromatic drinks do nothing to bring out the specific qualities of vodka. The aromas of the most sophisticated vodkas are overwhelmed by the other ingredients, which explains why the vodkas used in these mixed drinks are usually the most neutral and the least expensive to make. Their role is simply to add alcohol to the drink, and they can be mixed with almost any other ingredient, including more flavorful spirits like rum and whiskey.

But there are also fashions in cocktails, and today, a vodka cocktail evokes for many consumers a promise of exoticism.

CHI-CHI

Tall drink; serve as an aperitif
To a shaker half-filled with ice cubes, add:

- 3 PARTS VODKA
- 5 PARTS PINEAPPLE JUICE
- 2 PARTS COCONUT CREAM
- A DASH OF GRENADINE
- THE JUICE OF A LEMON

Shake well and pour into a champagne glass.

SOURIRE D'ANGE (ANGEL'S SMILE)

To a shaker half-filled with ice cubes, add:

- 3 PARTS VODKA
- 3 PARTS COINTREAU
- 3 PARTS KIRSCH
- 1 PART GRENADINE

Shake well and pour into a cocktail glass. Decorate with a preserved cherry.

Note: In spite of its deceptive sweetness, this is a rather strong after-dinner drink.

VOSLAU

Cocktail; serve after dinner
To a shaker half-filled with ice cubes, add:

- 5 PARTS VODKA
- 4 PARTS PEPPERMINT
- 1 PART MARASCHINO LIQUEUR
- A PINCH OF CAYENNE PEPPER

Shake well and pour into a cocktail glass.

BLACK RUSSIAN

To a glass containing a few ice cubes, add:

- 5 PARTS VODKA
- 5 PARTS KAHLUA (COFFEE LIQUEUR)

Mix well with a spoon.

Note: As its name indicates, this is a drink that warms the coldest nights, in Moscow and elsewhere. A Russian vodka is recommended.

BLOODY MARY

To a mixing glass containing a few ice cubes, add

- 2 PARTS VODKA
- 8 PARTS TOMATO JUICE
- 1 OR 2 DROPS OF TABASCO SAUCE
- A DASH OF WORCESTERSHIRE SAUCE
- CELERY SALT

Mix well with a spoon and pour into a tumbler. Decorate with a half-slice of lemon.

Note: The name of this classic drink refers to Mary Tudor, or "Bloody Mary," who persecuted the Protestants in the sixteenth century.

BLUE LAGOON

To a tumbler containing a few ice cubes, add:

- 6 PARTS VODKA
- 1 PART BLUE CURAÇAO
- 3 PARTS LEMON JUICE

Stir with a spoon and fill with sparkling water.

Note: Refreshing to both the eye and the taste buds, even though vodka has little connection to the South Seas.

ROMANOFF

Cocktail; serve after dinner
To a shaker half-filled with ice cubes, add:

- 9 PARTS VODKA
- 1 PART ANISETTE

Shake and pour into a cocktail glass. Decorate with a half-slice of lemon.

POMERANIA

Cocktail; serve as an aperitif
To a shaker half-filled with ice cubes, add:

- 6 PARTS VODKA
- 2 PARTS RED VERMOUTH
- 1 PART SUGAR SYRUP
- 1 PART LEMON JUICE

Shake vigorously and pour into a cocktail glass. Add lemon zest.

SNOWFLAKE

Tall drink; serve any time
To a shaker half-filled with ice cubes, add:

- 3 PARTS VODKA
- 1 PART GALLIANO LIQUEUR
- 1 PART SOUTHERN COMFORT
- 1 PART ADVOKAAT LIQUEUR
- 4 PARTS ORANGE JUICE

Shake for some time and pour into a large glass. Fill with soda and stir. Add liquid crème fraîche to the top and serve with a straw, decorated with an orange slice.

BULLSHOT

To a tumbler, add:

- 5 PARTS VODKA
- 5 PARTS COLD BEEF BOUILLON
- 2 DASHES OF WORCESTERSHIRE SAUCE
- 1 OR 2 DROPS OF TABASCO SAUCE
- A PINCH OF SALT

Mix well and decorate with a slice of lemon

Note: This is undeniably a British drink in spite of the use of vodka. A good pick-me-up after a night of over-indulgence.

MOSCOW MULE

Squeeze the juice of a lime into a large tumbler.

Add 5 centiliters (1.7 fluid ounces) of vodka and ice-cold ginger ale.

Mix with a spoon and add a slice of lime and a piece of cucumber peel.

Note: This recipe was popularized in the United States by a Smirnoff advertisement featuring Woody Allen. It's fun to have your guests make their own. Usually drunk in one gulp.

TROIKA

Cocktail; serve any time
To a shaker half-filled with ice cubes, add:

- 4 PARTS VODKA
- 3 PARTS LEMON JUICE
- 3 PARTS COINTREAU

Shake and pour into a cocktail glass.

TROPICAL STORM

Tall drink; serve any time
To a shaker half-filled with ice cubes, add:

- 2 PARTS VODKA
- 3 PARTS AMBER RUM
- 3 PARTS ORANGE JUICE
- 1 PART LIME JUICE
- 1 PART PINEAPPLE JUICE
- A DASH OF ANGOSTURA BITTERS
- 2 DASHES OF GRENADINE

Shake vigorously and pour into a large glass. Decorate with pieces of exotic fruit and serve with a straw.

CZARINA

To a mixing glass containing a few ice cubes, add:

- 5 PARTS VODKA
- 3 PARTS DRY WHITE VERMOUTH
- 2 PARTS APRICOT LIQUEUR
- A DASH OF ANGOSTURA BITTERS

Mix well with a spoon and pour into a cocktail glass.

Note: This cocktail of Russian origin requires a vodka with a high alcohol content and should be served as an after-dinner drink because of its strength.

GRAND PRIX

Cocktail; serve after dinner
To a shaker half-filled with ice cubes, add:

- 5 PARTS VODKA
- 3 PARTS DRY WHITE VERMOUTH
- 2 PARTS COINTREAU
- THE JUICE OF HALF A LEMON
- A DASH OF GRENADINE

Shake vigorously and pour into a cocktail glass.

SCREWDRIVER

To a glass containing a few ice cubes, add:

- 6 PARTS ORANGE JUICE
- 4 PARTS VODKA

Mix well and decorate with a half-slice of orange.

This is the classic drink that helped popularize vodka, especially among young people in discothèques.

APRES-SKI

*Tall drink;
serve any time*
To a shaker half-filled with ice cubes, add:

- 4 PARTS VODKA
- 3 PARTS PEPPERMINT
- 3 PARTS PERNOD

Shake and pour into a large glass. Fill with sparkling water, add a few ice cubes, and decorate with mint leaves.

WHITE SPIDER

To a glass containing a few ice cubes, add:

- 5 PARTS VODKA
- 5 PARTS COLORLESS MINT LIQUEUR

Mix with a spoon and decorate with a few mint leaves.

Note: This refreshing drink is made more surprising by the use of colorless mint liqueur.

GYPSY

To a shaker half filled with ice cubes, add:

- 6 PARTS VODKA
- 4 PARTS BENEDICTINE
- A DASH OF ANGOSTURA BITTERS

Shake well and pour into a cocktail glass.

Note: This fairly strong cocktail makes a good after-dinner drink.

GODMOTHER

To a glass containing a few ice cubes, add:

- 3 PARTS AMARETTO LIQUEUR
- 7 PARTS VODKA

Mix well.

Note: This rather strong cocktail with a pronounced flavor of almonds makes a good after-dinner drink.

BARBARA

Cocktail; serve after dinner
To a shaker half-filled with ice cubes, add:

- 5 PARTS VODKA
- 3 PARTS COCOA LIQUEUR
- 2 PARTS CRÈME FRAÎCHE

Shake vigorously and pour into a cocktail glass. Sprinkle lightly with cocoa.

GREENLAND

Tall drink; serve any time
To a shaker half-filled with ice cubes, add:

- 4 PARTS PINEAPPLE JUICE
- 3 PARTS VODKA
- 2 PARTS COINTREAU
- 1 PART LEMON JUICE

Shake, pour into a large tumbler, and fill with tonic water.

GULF STREAM

Cocktail; serve as an aperitif
To a shaker half-filled with ice cubes, add:

- 5 PARTS VODKA
- 5 PARTS GIN
- A DASH OF ANGOSTURA BITTERS

Shake briefly and pour into a cocktail glass. Add a green olive.

FLAMINGO

To a shaker half-filled with ice cubes, add:

- 6 PARTS VODKA
- 4 PARTS CAMPARI

Shake and pour into a champagne glass. Fill with champagne and decorate with an orange slice.

Note: This excellent aperitif should be consumed with moderation as it is stronger than it seems.

ZANZERAC

Cocktail; serve as an aperitif

To a mixing glass containing a few ice cubes, add:

- 4 PARTS VODKA
- 4 PARTS DRAMBUIE LIQUEUR
- 2 PARTS APRICOT LIQUEUR

Mix well and pour into a cocktail glass. Add a preserved cherry.

VODKATINI

To a mixing glass containing a few ice cubes, add:

- 8 PARTS VODKA
- 2 PARTS DRY WHITE VERMOUTH

Mix well with a spoon and pour into a cocktail glass. Add an olive.

Note: This is a vodka-based variation of the Dry Martini. To make it even more interesting, use a highly aromatic vodka, from Poland, for example.

CAPE CODDER

Tall drink; serve any time

To a tumbler containing a few ice cubes, add:

- 4 PARTS VODKA
- 6 PARTS BLUEBERRY JUICE
- THE JUICE OF HALF A LEMON

Mix well with a spoon and fill with sparkling water.

SPRINGTIME

To a shaker half filled with ice cubes, add:

- 5 PARTS VODKA
- 3 PARTS ORANGE JUICE
- 2 PARTS COINTREAU

Shake well and pour into a tumbler. Add soda or ginger ale and decorate with orange or lemon zest.

Note: A highly refreshing tall drink.

HARVEY WALLBANGER

Tall drink; serve any time

To a large tumbler containing a few ice cubes, add:

- 3 PARTS VODKA
- 7 PARTS ORANGE JUICE

Mix with a spoon and carefully add two tablespoons of Galliano liqueur on top of the drink. Decorate with a slice of orange and serve with a straw.

RED LIPS

Cocktail; serve after dinner

To a shaker half-filled with ice cubes, add:

- 5 PARTS VODKA
- 3 PARTS CAMPARI
- 2 PARTS GRAND MARNIER
- 1 EGG WHITE
- A DASH OF ANGOSTURA BITTERS

Shake for some time and pour into a cocktail glass.

VODKA COLLINS

To a tall glass, add:
- 5 CENTILITERS
  (1.7 OUNCES)
  VODKA
- 1 SPOONFUL OF
  SUGAR SYRUP
- THE JUICE OF A
  LEMON

Mix well with a spoon and fill with sparkling water. Serve with a straw.
Note: Less flavorful than a Tom Collins made with gin, this tall drink is just as refreshing.

SALTY DOG

Rub the rim of a large tumbler with lemon juice and dip in salt. Add ice cubes and:
- 3 PARTS VODKA
- 7 PARTS GRAPEFRUIT JUICE

Mix well before serving.
Note: The contrast between the salt and the acidity of the grapefruit juice makes this a very refreshing drink.

BLUE NIGHT

Cocktail; serve after dinner
To a shaker half-filled with ice cubes, add:
- 5 PARTS VODKA
- 3 PARTS GRAPEFRUIT JUICE
- 1 PART MALIBU
- 1 PART BARLEY WATER
- A DASH OF BLUE CURAÇAO

Shake vigorously and pour into a cocktail glass. Add a preserved cherry.

INDEX

of vodkas and aquavits

A

Aalborg, 118, 129
Ababycabl, 141
Absolut, 13, 19, 33, 46, 89, 93, 94, 95, 100-101, 102-103, 104-105, 106-107, 109, 137
Agros, 66
Altai, 34
Anisovaya, 48
Anton Brondum, 130
Après Ski, 154
Aquavit, 19, 89, 90, 118, 120, 122-123, 124-125, 126-127, 128-129, 130-131, 132-133, 151
Arcus, 120, 133
Artic, 143

B

Bacardi, 136, 141
Baikalskaya, 48
Baltic, 72
Barbara, 155
Barowa, 72
Bénédictine, 142
Bialowesia, 61, 86
Bielska, 72
Bismarck, 141
Black Currant, 74
Black Death, 142
Black Russian, 57, 153
Bloody Mary, 41, 57, 139, 153
Blue lagoon, 153
Blue Night, 157
Boyard, 26
Brännvin, 89, 90, 91, 95, 96, 100
Brondum Kummen, 129
Brown Forman, 102
Bullshot, 57, 153
Burnett's, 138

C

Campbell, 141
Cape Codder, 156
Carillon, 46, 102, 104, 106
Cheveleff, 115`
Chi-Chi, 152
Chopin, 74
Chymos, 115
CK Vodka, 67
Crater Lake, 138
Cristall, 12, 35
Cytronowka, 74
Czardasz, 77
Czarina, 154

D

Danisco Distillers, 118, 119, 129
Danzka Vodka, 119
De Hoorn, 143
Degtiné, 122
Dethleffesen, 141
Devil's Spring, 138
Dovgan, 31, 36, 39
Dry Vodka, 112

E

Eesti Viin, 122
Eristoff, 136, 141
Everclear, 138
Explorer, 95

F

Favorits, 122
Finlandia, 13, 109, 110, 111
Flamingo, 155
Flocon de neige, 153
Friis Vodka, 119
Frost, 138

G

Gamal Norrlands, 133
Gilbey's, 58, 138, 142
Gipsy, 155
Glacier Bay, 138
Gnesnania Boonekamp, 68, 77
Godmother, 155
Gorbatschow, 136, 140
Gordon's, 138, 142
Grand prix, 154
Grant's, 141, 143
Grey Goose, 142
Groënland, 155
Gulf Stream, 155

H

Hammer, 120
Harald Jansen, 130
Hartwig-Kantorowicz, 68
Harvey Wallbanger, 156
Henius (Isidor), 118, 126, 129
Henkell, 141
Heublein, 33, 54, 55, 57, 58, 135
Hiram Walker, 102, 119
Holger Denske, 130
Hunter, 77
Hussar, 143

I

IB Berentzen, 141
Ice Hotel, 104, 106
IDV, 33
Inferno, 139
Irish Distillers, 143
Izy, 97

J

J&J Nordic, 97
Jägar, 95
Jarzebiak, 77
Jim Beam, 140

K

Karinskaya, 141
Karkov, 137
Karl Marx, 141
Karpatia, 79
Kasprowicz, 68
Kasztelanska, 79
Keglevich, 143
Ketel One, 143
Kitting Ridge, 139
Koskenkorva, 109, 112
Krakus, 68, 79
Kremlyovskaya, 39
Krepkaya, 39
Kristal Dzidrais, 122
Krolewska, 79
Kron, 95
Krupnik, 147, 150
Kubanskaya, 39
Kunnett (Rudolph), 54, 55, 57, 58,

L

Lancut, 10, 21, 15, 64, 65, 66, 67, 68, 78, 79
Langow, 33
Lanique, 79
Leader, 141
Legend, 141
Leijonaviina, 112
Lignell & Piispanen, 112, 115
Limonnaya, 39
Liudka, 143
Liviko Distilleries, 122
Lodowa, 68
Loiten Export, 133
Luksusowa, 81
Lysholm, 133
Lysholm Linie, 133

M

Maccahapa Zarskaya
Datscha, 48

Mad River, 138
Marli, 115
Martin (John), 54, 55, 56, 58
Martini, 141, 142
Maximus, 112
Monopole, 122
Monopolowa, 81, 82
Monopols, 122
Moscow mule, 56, 154
moskovskaia ossobia, 32
Moskovskaya, 35, 41, 45
Mounier, 142

N

Nolet, 143
Nordfors viina, 115
Nyköpings, 95

O

Okhotnichya, 41
Old Warrior, 141
Orage tropical, 154
Oskar Davidsen, 130

P

Pernod-Ricard, 34, 141
Pertsovka, 41
Pieprzowka, 82
Piolunowka, 141
Pohjan Poika Vodka, 115
Polish Pure Spirit, 82
Polmos, 17, 65, 66, 69, 74, 78, 86
Polonaise, 68, 83
Pomeraine, 153
Pontikka, 115
Popov, 138
Posnanian, 68
Posolskaya, 48
Potocki (Alfred), 64, 67, 68
Pöytaviina, 112
Poznań (Distilleries de), 68, 72, 77, 78, 81, 83
Premium, 68, 83
Primalco, 112
Prince Igor, 139
Priviet, 42
Pshenichnaya, 42
Pusckin, 141

R

Rain, 138
Rajamäki, 108, 109, 110
Rasputin, 141
Red Lips, 156
Remedia, 122
Renat, 95
Rigalya, 122
Rigas Originalais, 122
Riistaryyppy, 112
Romanoff, 153
Rouss, 34
Royalty, 143
Russkaya, 42

S

Sahti-Mafia, 115
Saint-Petersbourg, 48
Salty Dog, 157
samogon, 30
Saturnus, 95
Screwdriver, 57, 154
Seagram, 102, 106
Selekt, 142
Sibirskaya, 42
Silver Creek, 138
Skåne Akvavit, 133
Skky, 139, 140
Smirnoff, 11, 12, 13, 33, 42, 46, 52-53, 54-55, 56-57, 58-59, 67, 84, 135, 136, 138, 140
Smirnoff Black, 42, 58
Smirnoff Silver, 140
Smirnov, 11, 12, 21, 23, 27
Smirnov (Boris), 33, 58, 59
Smirnov (Piotr Arsenyevitch), 11, 13, 42, 52, 53, 58, 59
Smirnov (Vladimir Petrovitch), 53, 54, 136
Smith (Lars Olsson), 93, 100, 102, 104
Soïouzplodimport, 31, 33, 46
Soplica, 83
Sourire d'ange, 152
Spring Time, 156
Star of Russia, 48
Starka, 45, 83
Stock, 143
Stolbovaya, 48

Stolichnaya, 33, 35, 45, 46, 138
Stolovaya, 46
Strovia, 48
Strzelczyk, 68
Suntory, 119
Svensk Vodka, 96, 97

T

Tähkäviina, 112
Tanqueray, 142
Tatra, 84
TBWA, 104, 105, 106, 138
Teton River, 138
Troïka, 154
Turowka, 86

U

Ultra, 46
Ursus, 143

V

Vikingfjord, 120
Viktoria, 48
Viljavaakuna, 112
Vin&Sprit, 91, 94, 95, 102, 133
Virgin, 135, 142
Viru Valge, 122
Vistula, 84
Vladivar, 142
Vodka Collins, 157
Vodkatini, 58, 156
Voslau, 152

W

White Spider, 155
Whyte and Mackay, 142
Wisent, 65, 67, 86
Wisniowka, 150
Wisniowska, 84
Woda, 62
Wodka Krolewska, 69
Wolfschmidt, 140
Wyborowa, 68, 69, 84, 86

Y

Yubileynaya, 48

Z

Zakouski, 23, 147
Zanzerac, 156
Zelta, 122
Zielona Gora, 69, 74, 78, 79, 83
Ziolowa Mocna, 86
Zlota woda, 64
Zoladkova Gorzka, 86
Zolotoe Koltso, 48
Zubrovka, 48
Zubrowka, 12, 69, 86, 151
Zucco, 143
Zytnia, 86, 147

PHOTO CREDITS